New Brand
Leadership

NEW BRAND LEADERSHIP

Managing at the Intersection of Globalization, Localization, and Personalization

Larry Light
Joan Kiddon

Publisher: Paul Boger
Editor-in-Chief: Amy Neidlinger
Operations Specialist: Jodi Kemper
Cover Designer: Alan Clements
Managing Editor: Kristy Hart
Senior Project Editor: Lori Lyons
Copy Editor: Gill Editorial Services
Proofreader: Paula Lowell
Indexer: Lisa Stumpf
Compositor: Nonie Ratcliff
Manufacturing Buyer: Dan Uhrig

For information about buying this title in bulk quantities, or for special sales opportunities (which may include electronic versions; custom cover designs; and content particular to your business, training goals, marketing focus, or branding interests), please contact our corporate sales department at corpsales@pearsoned.com or (800) 382-3419.

For government sales inquiries, please contact governmentsales@pearsoned.com.

For questions about sales outside the U.S., please contact international@pearsoned.com.

Printed in the United States of America

First Printing: June 2015

ISBN-10: 0-13-419382-2
ISBN-13: 978-0-13-419382-3

Pearson Education LTD.
Pearson Education Australia PTY, Limited.
Pearson Education Singapore, Pte. Ltd.
Pearson Education Asia, Ltd.
Pearson Education Canada, Ltd.
Pearson Educación de Mexico, S.A. de C.V.
Pearson Education—Japan
Pearson Education Malaysia, Pte. Ltd.

Library of Congress Control Number: 2015936074

We dedicate this book to the Mars family—Forrest Mars Jr., John Mars and Jackie Mars, as well as the senior executives Howard Walker and Claude-Elliott Herman—who offered us the first opportunity to work as global brand marketers.

Not only were they passionate about their brands, but they had the foresight and vision to lead the way in addressing global marketing challenges and opportunities.

Working with Mars, Inc., as our first global client, we began to craft many of the ideas that have evolved into our enduring principles for global brand management.

Contents

Acknowledgments

Special thanks goes to our families for continuing to put up with us and encourage us and love us...Joyce, Laura, and Michelle Light, Chloé and Olivia Kiddon, and Naomi Levine.

About the Authors

Larry Light is the Chairman and CEO of Arcature. Larry was Global CMO of McDonald's from 2002 to 2005. More recently, as the interim Global Chief Brands Officer of IHG from 2011 to 2013, Larry led global organizational and marketing process change to increase the effectiveness of IHG's global and local marketing. Light was formerly the Executive Vice President at BBDO and was Chairman and CEO of the international division of Bates Worldwide and was also a member of the Bates' Board of Directors. In 2004, *Brandweek* selected Larry as one of the top ten marketers of the year and McDonald's won "Marketer of the Year" from *Advertising Age*. In its report on Best Marketers of the Decade, *AdWeek* reported that "Larry Light, who turned around McDonald's as CMO from 2002 to 2005 finished second to Steve Jobs." Summarizing the top ten ideas of the decade, *Ad Age* selected Larry Light's "Brand Journalism" as "arguably the most realistic description of marketing today—perhaps ever." In 2013, in partnership with the Association of National Advertisers, the *Internationalist* recognized Larry among 100 marketing leaders from around the world who are consistently moving business forward.

Joan Kiddon is President and COO of Arcature. Joan began her career in 1976 as a market researcher at BBDO Worldwide in New York. In 1978, she moved into Account Management. She was the head of marketing and market research for BBDO West, Los Angeles, from 1980 until 1986. In 1990, she joined Arcature. Joan consulted to McDonald's during its brand turnaround from 2002 until 2005. Kiddon with Light consulted to IHG from 2010 to 2014. Joan Kiddon is the co-author of *Six Rules for Brand Revitalization: Learn How Companies Like McDonald's Can Re-Energize Their Brands*.

Introduction

This is an exciting and transformative time to be in marketing. The energy and innovativeness of marketing can create and tackle the dynamics of our shifting and shaking environment to become the central power of brand-business management. Many of the important factors that are changing our world are also affecting the way we build and manage brands.

First, three forces—globalization, localization, and personalization—are increasing simultaneously. To be winners, brands must learn to leverage all three of these powerful energies to their advantage. The world is increasingly connected, but relevant regional differences cannot be ignored, and personalized experiences build preference whether delivered by humans, by technology, or through a combination of both.

Second, there is the demographic challenge of our world becoming older and younger at the same time. We continue to experience the influence of the aging (and longer living) baby boomers with the simultaneous growing influence of the millennial generation.

Third, people have conflicting desires for individuality and inclusivity. They want to be respected as individuals, but they also want to belong to communities of people with whom they share common interests.

Fourth, technology has an increased effect on customer behavior and the power of a mobile mind-set. In particular, the increased use of mobile and the immediacy of customer information are affecting decision-making behaviors.

Fifth, trust in institutions continues to decline. Consumers trust the opinions of unknown reviewers rather than the opinions of brands or experts. The original touchstones of trust such as schools, governments, religions, legal systems, and businesses have lost credibility and have been replaced by real or virtual families, friends, and peers.

All these factors are increasing at different speeds but at the same time. How do we build powerful brands in this complex, dynamic, changing world? In particular, how do we build strong brands in a world that is becoming more global, more local and more personal all at the same time? These challenges demand that we revisit the way global brands are managed. They require a new approach to organizational account-abilities and the way we work together. Global brands bring us coherence, reliability, certainty, and they address universal truths such as hunger, family status, performance, and acceptance. By virtue of the fact that they cross geography, global brands are not of one single place. Local brands bring us relevance to help us understand place—our communities, neighborhoods, homes, and countries. Local brands bind us together as belonging to particular places whether physical or virtual. Being personal defines each of us as an individual: personality says who we are, differentiating us from others. Global, local, and personal must be managed for brands to be successful.

Through our 45 years of experience on the agency, consulting, and client sides with line authority, we have learned there is a better way to build strong global brands. Over the years, we have developed and put into practice the principles of The Collaborative Three-Box Model: the better way to organize and market global brands.

The Collaborative Three-Box Model is a solution to the many challenges in global brand marketing and a better way forward in an ever-changing world. The Model is flexible, responsive, and relevant. More importantly, it addresses the organizational and mind-set issues that create hurdles to effective global brand marketing. Its implications are wide-ranging across and throughout the enterprise. The Model is a new mind-set driving change in behaviors and, in some cases, reorganization of the enterprise.

The global marketing challenge is to build strong brands that are globally consistent, locally relevant, and personally differentiated. Our Model based on shared responsibility provides marketing muscle so organizations can have the strength and power to compete both effectively and efficiently.

What are the elements that we see as drivers behind the creation of our new approach to global brand marketing? This book covers a lot of territory because there are so many different things happening on so many levels, including interpersonal relationships, brand relationships, information availability, and technology. Our view is highly integrative: the various trends, forces, and perceptions are now woven together to provide a new context for marketing brands. Corporate and brand strategies will need to change; organizations will need some realignments; products and services will need to become more focused and more flexible.

This book is organized into three parts:

- **Part I: The Changing Context for Global Brand Marketing—** This describes the changing world and sets up the vital and volatile context for The Collaborative Three-Box Model.

  We take note of a key demographic development affecting marketing: the world is getting older and younger at the same time. We also observe the massive collision of three forces: increased globalization, increased localization, and increased personalization. We see the rise of a phenomenon we call Inclusive Individuality and the rise of hyper-connectivity. And, increasingly, customers are more and more skeptical. Trust is in decline.

- **Part II: The Collaborative Three-Box Model—**This offers a detailed description of the Model and what people need to do and not do to make it work worldwide.

  The changing marketing world will require a change in how marketing is organized: new roles, new responsibilities, and new accountabilities. Effective brand management requires collaboration across global, regional, and cross-functional teams.

- **Part III: Refreshing the Enterprise—**This part is about gaining alignment for action and measuring progress on behalf of strong global brands.

How do we achieve organizational alignment around a common brand vision while building local brand relevance? And what global and local metrics do we use to measure progress?

This book looks at the evolution of global brand marketing and sets the context for why now is the critical time for an immediate change in marketing approach. We explain, through specific examples, how to put these concepts into action and how to allocate organizational responsibilities so as to overcome the natural tensions between global and local teams We also discuss how this new approach helps to generate increased brand value. The Collaborative Three-Box Model is the modern way to organize for global brands. It is a process, an organizational structure, and a mind-set designed to help brands manage in a 24/7 complex business, cultural, social, and economic environment. The ideas in this book provide global brands with an actionable blueprint for a working knowledge of the issues that arise from the tensions of global and local decision rights, the role of the center relative to the role of the regions, and the specific idea that brand leadership is global and brand management is local.

Larry Light

Joan Kiddon

PART I

The Changing Context for Global Brand Marketing

1

Overview: A New Approach to Global Marketing

"[Globalization] represents the world's best chance to enrich the lives of the greatest number of people."

—William Wishard

Raising the Issues

It was a short letter to the editor of the *New York Times* that pushed a "hot-button" on the issue of globalization. On May 27, 2014, the *New York Times* published a letter that described the value of globalization if managed appropriately. The letter writer suggested that globalization provides us "awareness as a single entity." He wrote "...if pursued wisely, it represents the world's best chance to enrich the lives of the greatest number of people."[1]

Embedded in the letter was an additional thought that is at the center of an ongoing debate: "How can we engage in globalization without losing our traditions?"[2] In other words, how can we be global, local, and personal at the same (see Figure 1.1)? Although the letter was not about marketing, the issue is extremely relevant...and frustrating...to marketers who must ensure that the global brands they promote are locally relevant and personally differentiated.

Marketers continue to discuss the balance of global and local. Graystone Consulting, one of the many businesses of Morgan Stanley, proudly states in its advertising: "Local Presence or Global Powerhouse (Pick Two) Discover the best of both worlds."[3]

Figure 1.1 Collision of global forces

The Globalization of Marketing

For a long time, being locally relevant was not considered to be necessary for brands except for language and monetary currencies. Ever since Ted Levitt wrote his seminal article, "The Globalization of Marketing," in 1983 for the *Harvard Business Review*,[4] global marketing has been dominated by the standardization of products, services, brands, and standardized communications worldwide. Professor Levitt made a strong case for the increased efficiency of brand globalization. He believed ubiquitous, uniform global brand marketing would be more profitable.

Clearly, thinking has changed. Today, in our highly connected, over-informed, technology-driven world, people have a love-hate relationship with globalization. They appreciate the comfort and reliability of recognized, iconic brands anywhere they go on the planet. Yet they bemoan the homogenization of products and services and yearn for the authentic, locally occurring experiences now sacrificed at the altar of sameness. Although customers want the safety, security, and predictability of global brands, they also feel that global brands are powerful behemoths that simply do not understand who they are as individuals.

They see global organizations as threats to local economies, cultures, communities, and the environment.

From a business perspective, as pointed out recently in the press, older globalization business models based on size and clout are fading fast in the face of nimbleness and agility. These existing operations are susceptible to the revolutionary technology and optimism of a new digital globalization.[5]

Localism

There is a growing tension between globalism and localism. In today's world, the rise in power of nationalism is visible and palpable. Nationalism disguised as localism is so prevalent that a senior advisor at Nomura spoke on Bloomberg TV about the role of nationalism in the current global crises and in governmental policies from the Middle East, Ukraine, Hong Kong, France, Sweden, and the UK.[6]

This same tension is being felt within business organizations. "My region is different. I am accountable for my market. I will develop and implement my plan for my market." These are common attitudes fighting against common goals.

In the issue, *The World in 2015*, *The Economist* suggested, "nationalism is the most enduring of the -isms that begat so many wars in the 20th Century." "Democratic countries that wish to preserve their unity would be wise to devolve and decentralize." Spain, Canada, and Scotland are the ones mentioned.[7]

When the world becomes shaky politically, economically, and socially, it affects global businesses. Organic farmers in Russia are experiencing more interest in locally grown food and food provenance now that global sanctions against Russia have raised prices for regularly grown foodstuffs: "The main thing which the sanctions have already changed is in people's minds—in government, in business and on the streets, they have started to think more about where their food comes from," Boris Ackimov, artisanal cheese maker and founder of Russia's farm-to-table movement.[8]

Personalization

It is no longer just a conflict between globalization and localization. Now there is the added force of targeted, micro personalization. People want and expect branded experiences that are highly personalized. This addition of personal differentiation introduces a third dimension and a major complexity to the global-local tension.

The colliding forces of increased globalization, localization, and personalization present a challenge for global brands and the organizations that own them: how to manage brands in the midst of these three simultaneous forces. With the amazing surge in technology, consumers appreciate 1) the efficiency and familiarity benefits of globalization, 2) brands that reflect and respect local differences, and 3) the personalization of products and services.

Global brand management needs a new approach for "managing to win" across geography and time. The old-think global brand marketing approaches must be replaced by a twenty-first century mind-set and discipline that reflects these current issues.

Global brands need a way of handling these dynamics while needing the organizational structure to leverage the opportunities that are present.

Game-Changers

What are the game-changers that marketers must consider when creating and implementing strategies? What are those trends that are presently having a huge impact on consumers? Although there are many trends, we focus on five. These five are having and will continue to have impact on global marketing and on how we create, nurture, and strengthen global brands.

Whether you own or manage a large global brand or a small local brand, understanding these five trends and creating and executing programs to leverage them are marketing and brand survival imperatives.

1. **The two-humped demographic camel**—Demographics are a marketing reality. The world is getting older and younger at the same time with Boomers (born between 1946 and 1964) at one end of the spectrum and Millennials (born between 1982 and

2000) at the other. It is popular in the current marketing environment to focus primarily on Millennials. The real issue is that over the next decade, marketers will have to be relevant to two huge groups of people who have different values and view the world through different lenses (see Figure 1.2).

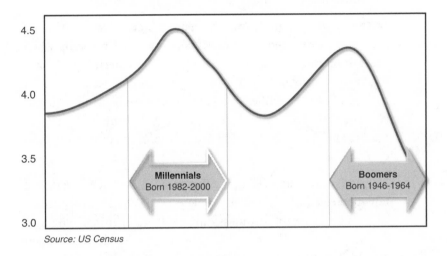

Source: US Census

Figure 1.2 The two-humped demographic camel

2. **Personalization is on the rise**—Personalization is different from customization. Customization is transactional and all about features and functions; personalization is experiential. Technology is fueling this desire for the ever-more-personalized experience. Personalization can be delivered in many ways, and Millennials and Boomers have different sets of expectations. The dark side of personalization needs to be taken into account because there is a fine line between insightful personalization and intrusive prying. Millennials and Boomers see this invasion of privacy differently.

3. **The evolution from the Age of We to the Age of Me to the Age of I**—There is a new values mind-set in which people want to be individuals while being part of like-minded communities of common interests. The Age of We was the golden era of mass marketing beginning after World War II. The Age of Me was the flowering of the Boomer culture. It was a self-focused,

self-indulgent "me generation" era where the individual ruled. Today, we live in the Age of I—the Inclusive Individualists. Technology is driving the ability to belong to many different groups, each reflecting a part of you while desiring to be perceived as an independent person. It's changing the nature of relationships, communities, and family.

4. **In the techno, digital, mobile instant, networked world, we are hyper-connected**—Closeness takes on a new meaning when you are physically not close. Family has new meanings. I have my "real" family with whom I can stay in contact 24/7, and I have my created families: the communities of like-minded others. The proliferation of data, technology, and multiple devices requires marketers to build brand relationships differently than ever before.

5. **The decline in trust**—So many things that were once so right are now perceived as having let people down. Whether institutions such as government, business, universities, organized religions, finance, or advertising and brands, trust is in decline. When people do not trust you or your brand or your organization, they doubt you will deliver on your promises. Doubt is driving skepticism, frustration, and even anger. Studies show that increasingly customers are more and more skeptical. As a result, some are becoming increasingly activist. The Edelman Trust Barometer and global research by Monitor and other studies indicate a lack of trust in big enterprises and a growth in doubt and anger.[9]

Of these forces, personalization is already the major game-changer. Although all three forces—globalization, localization, and personalization—are important for global brand marketing, the rise of personalization seems to be having the biggest impact on what we expect from brands and how we perceive them. Companies such as Blue Nile (online diamond jeweler), Birchbox (monthly subscription service of personalized beauty products), Trunk Club (Men's personalized shopping and delivery service), and Stitch Fix (personalized styling service for women) are creating product and service experiences designed for the individual customer.[10] Customers increasingly desire products and services that reflect personal wants and needs. Trust is critical.

All brands are relationship based. A brand is a bond—a promise that you will deliver what you promise. As with any relationship, trust allows for belief that the other party will do what's promised. Trust affects the perceived value of a brand. To create more personalized products and services, brands need to know details about the customer. The more customers trust, the more they will share personal information. The more information shared, the more intensely personal the experiences.

Changed Perception of Value

The game-changing trends are affecting customers' branded experiences because expectations have changed. Altered expectations change the customer's approach to assessing the value of a brand. Marketers have been their own worst enemies by letting the idea of "value" become a substitute for "low price." Value can happen at any price point: "That's a great value" can apply to a Mercedes and a Kia; it can apply to a shoe from Designer Shoe Warehouse and from Saks Fifth Avenue. It applies to Aldi supermarkets and to Harrods food court. Value is in the eye of the customer, and it is learned from interaction. The trends and forces affecting brands have now affected changes to the way in which customers perceive brand value.

Trustworthy Brand Value

Today, there is a new customer-perceived brand value equation that we'll call *Trustworthy Brand Value*. Trust is an important factor in this equation. For the customer, what you get (functional, emotional, and social benefits) for what you pay (the costs to the customer in terms of money, time, and effort) creates brand value. Trust acts as a multiplier when consumers take mental assessments of a brand's worth. Without trust, brands have little value. This is the new value equation. Understanding its drivers will be one of the greatest opportunities for brands. Trustworthy Brand Value needs to become embedded within the organization and its brands. It needs to be part of the daily brand discussion. Are we increasing or decreasing our brand's Trustworthy Brand Value? Can we measure it? What must we do, continue to do, or stop doing to increase Trustworthy Brand Value? One of the goals we have for our new approach to global marketing is to ensure that it creates, nurtures, builds, and grows Trustworthy Brand Value.

Build Trust

We live in a "Disordered World," as Richard Haass wrote in *Foreign Affairs*.[11] This geopolitical unraveling has several sources, and lack of trust in our global partners and governments is one of them. It is the same for global brands, whether corporate brands or product or service brands. In fact, institutions everywhere are increasingly less trusted year to year. Building trust as a source of organizational wealth is an important driver for enduring, profitable growth. As we show with the new value equation, trust is a value multiplier. As trust increases, so does brand value. If there is no trust, there is no value. Creating Trust Capital allows a company or a brand to generate a trust reserve that helps through crises of brand or corporate character. A trust reserve of Trust Capital builds strong relationships over time.

The Collaborative Three-Box Model

As we track the evolution of the customer's perception of value, we also trace the evolution of global marketing. The changes of global brand marketing go from 1) the global standardization approach: a one-box model where the focus is on brand globalization; to 2) the "Think Globally. Act Locally." mantra: a two-box model where the center created the strategy and the regions were responsible executing the global strategy; to our approach, 3) The Collaborative Three-Box Model, today's most relevant approach (see Figure 1.3).

The Model is structured as follows:

- Box 1: Create the brand vision.
- Box 2: Define the global brand plan to win.
- Box 3: Bring the brand to life.

Although the new model may feel intuitively correct, it is not so easy to implement. This is because The Collaborative Three-Box Model is more than a process; it is a mind-set change, a leadership change, with a change of corporate focus and structure.

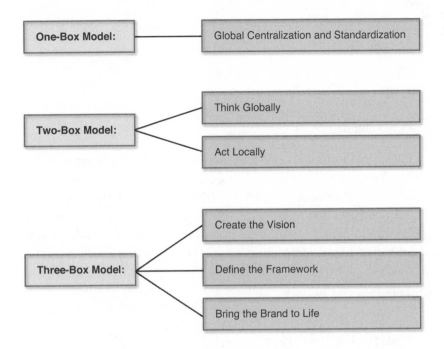

Figure 1.3 Approaches to global marketing

For The Collaborative Three-Box approach to work, global and regional teams need to collaborate. Effective collaboration requires cross-functional teams (CFTs). CFTs break down silos and stimulate productive discussions and actions. Carlos Ghosn initiated CFTs as a critical ingredient in the Nissan turnaround.[12] Collaboration is difficult when the organization is highly centralized or highly decentralized. Our marketing approach requires a new method for evaluation and metrics that define accountabilities. Instead of teams that are coalitions of the willing (prepared and considering to do something), brands today need coalitions of collaboration (working jointly together).

This new approach looks at the role of the center as the place for Global Brand Leadership. Global Brand Leadership is a combination of five factors:

1. Inspiration
2. Education
3. Influence
4. Support
5. Evaluation

In many organizations, "who is responsible for brand performance" is one of the most divisive issues. Is it the center? Is it the regions? Where does accountability reside? Most organizations are burdened with brand structures that reflect a different world. These outdated ideas of global brand management are a holdover from decades-old marketing theories. In an environment of the three colliding forces, relevant, productive, global brand management has to evolve from old-think to new-think marketing.

Creating the Metrics

Is The Collaborative Three-Box Model working? Are we making progress toward the brand vision? Are our actions within the Global Brand Framework building brand preference and brand familiarity, creating trustworthy brand value and quality revenue growth, and increasing profit? Some of the goals of this book are to help you focus on the essential metrics and the creation of a Brand Business Scorecard. This means knowing and being facile with the metrics of brand progress; in other words, how are we doing? The output of The Collaborative Three-Box Model is funneled into a Brand Business Scorecard. How are we doing in terms of getting closer to our goals? Are we improving? Achievements are good, but it is equally important to see how close we are getting to our brand's ambition. Having a common scorecard creates a platform for accountability, consistency, and cooperation.

Plan to Win

One of the most important tools in the new approach to global branding is the Plan to Win. The Plan to Win is a brand roadmap that aligns all business units and functions around the same goals, actions, and measures. It is a common platform for building Trustworthy Brand Value. It contains the necessary components of success and creates a common language that is consistent and clear within the organization. And, because everyone is following the same roadmap, the Plan to Win helps to break down the silos of isolationism. We will focus on what is entailed in developing an effective Plan to Win. This means creating the necessary internal discipline while never dispensing with the intuitive understanding of the brand.

Gaining Alignment: Overcoming the Negatives

Over the decades, we learned that many organizations share the same problematic issues when it comes to building brands. It is not unusual to hear clients in different industries complain about the same recurring problems. From our perspective, these problems or "bad habits" can get in the way of making The Collaborative Three-Box Model work. However, there are solutions. What are some of the organizational, cultural, and mind-set hurdles that need to be overcome to quickly move forward with The Model? Think of these as the "stop doing" behaviors or the "Avoid" behaviors. There is always work to be done when it comes to changing some of an organization's "ways of doing business." Face the facts; fix the fractures and then formulate for the future.

What Can I Do Differently?

What do we have to do differently to build Trust Capital, leverage the significant trends, and address the new value equation, Trustworthy Brand Value? What behaviors and attitudes will need to change? The old adage that actions speak louder than words is not a cliché but reality. To support the concepts discussed in this book, we provide a set of Guiding Principles. The Guiding Principles will help when it comes to breaking the bad habits. Business books and executive and organizational trainers emphasize that change is always difficult. To master and win with the new approach to handling and growing global brands, collaboration is key. Collaboration in many cases can be even more difficult than change. It means working together with people and functions with which you have remained separate. It means giving up control of things that you have previously controlled. The highlighted Guiding Principles help organizations work through the stumbling blocks of collaboration.

Aligning for Action

To sum up our thinking, we focus on organizational alignment. People need to be in agreement embracing the changes. The Collaborative Three-Box Model applies to all functions, not just marketing. Although it is in essence a marketing approach, because it deals with brands, all functions will at some point participate. Making acolytes out of acceptors is the only way to create winning brands.

Following a speech at the Association of National Advertisers in March of 2013, we introduced The Collaborative Three-Box Model in an article for the *Journal of Brand Strategy* in the Summer 2013 issue.[13] After its publication, David Aaker reported on the article on his blog. David is a best-selling brand-business author, a respected professor, and a recognized authority on brand management. He said,

> "A key device to carrying out this change will be a cross-functional and cross-geographical team that will be able to work in a defined context to provide inclusion for local brand teams.... Another is the concept of a matrix organization.... Matrix roles are not easy to make work. But, according to Larry, they are a fact of life in the global organization.
>
> Larry has clearly indicated that a shared responsibility should be the end goal of global brand strategy teams. It makes sense, but making it happen might not be easy."[14]

Brand Journalism

One way to leverage the trifecta of global-local-personal is to adopt an approach we call *Brand Journalism*. Brand Journalism generates a lot of press today. Many companies adopted it to deal with a world of different people who have multiple communications devices.

Brand Journalism is an engaging, multifaceted, flexible way of communicating a dynamic, evolving brand story. It means telling the many facets of the brand story to different people in different ways without ever losing the focus on what is known and loved about the brand. Brand Journalism addresses the fact that a brand means different things in different regions to different people in different situations. It keeps the brand's core characteristics intact while expressing the brand's different aspects through different branded communications across multiple devices and media. It is based on the concept that no single communication can ever tell a brand's entire story.

Making The Collaborative Three-Box Model a Reality

The Collaborative Three-Box Model is more than a marketing approach. It is a process change, a mind-set change, an organizational cultural change. When an organization follows the principles and steps of The Model, global brands can maximize being globally coherent, locally relevant, and personally unique.

It is not easy. It is not a simple, centralized brand dictatorship where the center disseminates thought and action. Nor is it a two-step, partitioned "Think globally...Act locally..." hand-off of responsibilities. The Model levels the playing field between global and regional teams by maximizing their proper roles and possibilities.

The global brand winners will be the ones that build great global brands that are locally relevant and personally differentiated. Our shared responsibility Model provides marketing muscle so organizations can have brand strength and power to compete both effectively and efficiently.

Endnotes

1. Wishard, William A., "Letter to the Editor," *New York Times*, May 27, 2014.

2. Ibid.

3. Print advertising campaign for Graystone Consulting, 2014, Morgan Stanley Smith Barney LLC.

4. Levitt, Theodore, "The Globalization of Marketing," *Harvard Business Review*, May/June, 1983.

5. Schumpeter column, "Mammom's Manichean turn," *The Economist*, January 31, 2015.

6. Ferro, Jonathan, *On the Move*, Bloomberg TV, October 31, 2014.

7. Grimond, John, "Splitting Images," *The World in 2015, The Economist*, November 2014, p. 31.

8. MacFarquahar, Neil, "Organic Farms Become a Winner in Putin's Feud with the West," *New York Times*, November 19, 2014.

9. Edelman Trust Barometer, 2014 Annual Global Study, Edelman, 2014. And Global Monitor, The Futures Company, 2013.

10. Wood, Molly, "Shopping with Data, and Adding a Human Touch," *New York Times*, August 14, 2014.

11. Haass, Richard N., "How to Respond to a Disordered World," *Foreign Affairs*, November-December 2014, Vol. 93, No. 6, pp. 70–79.

12. Ghosn, Carlos with Philippe Ries, *Shift: Inside Nissan's Historic Revival*, December 2005.

13. Light, Larry, "How Organizations Manage Global Brands in an Increasingly Local World," *The Journal of Brand Strategy*, Henry Stewart Publications, Vol. 2, No. 3, Summer 2013.

14. Aaker, David, "Collaborative Global Brand Management Is the Answer, According to Larry Light," David Aaker Blog, http://www.prophet.com, January 22, 2014.

2

Globalization, Localization, Personalization

In the kaleidoscope of chaos
The headline reads:
"We're going to extremes"
Are we a reflection, of life?
(It's a) long, long way from here to there
Kaleidoscope of chaos

—Paul Van Dyk[1]

We Are Already Affected by the Three Forces

Every day, we experience the effects of globalization, localization, and personalization. We buy clothes made in Asia. We see protesters at WTO events. We understand and possibly participate in the farm-to-table movement buying locally produced products. We like the locally brewed beer and the artisans from our own backyards. We read content that is personalized just for our tastes. Messages designed specifically for each of us capture our attention. Multiple times a day we are exposed to global, local, and personal events and messages, products, and services. We are caught up in social economic, political, marketing chaos caused by the collision of three powerful forces: globalization, localization, and personalization.

These three forces that have been evolving for many decades are now coming together in a whirlwind. They are the foundation for why our world seems so chaotic at times, especially for marketers where the road-map is unclear and there is no GPS. The Collaborative Three-Box Model is the recommended roadmap defining the way forward. According to Alex Pentland, "Suddenly our society has become a combination of humans and technology that has powers and weaknesses different from any we have ever lived in before."[2]

The way we manage brands needs to change. We will discuss the evolution of global brand marketing later in this book, but it is worth explaining here why this sweeping, pan-geography background is making The Collaborative Three-Box Model a marketing imperative.

The Collision of Three Forces

Globalization, localization, and personalization shape how brands must be managed. These three dynamics are colliding now. The challenge for marketers is to harness the strengths of each to build strong brands. This will require enterprise structure and mind-set changes as well as changes to the operational systems, policies, and processes used for brands. It will require a more meaningful, relevant, systematic, disciplined set of strategies for effective brand building.

The Collaborative Three-Box Model is a guide to how brand owners can succeed in this collision, turning mayhem into opportunity. Working together as a three-legged stool, these forces give focus, relevance, and sensitivity to brands. They are a wide-angle lens and a portrait lens rolled into one. Globalization delivers a familiar, consistent, and reliable branded experience. Localization delivers a relevant and respectful branded experience. Finally, personalization delivers a branded experience that recognizes and reflects the customer and is exclusively designed to meet an individual's needs for a particular occasion. Success in the twenty-first century will depend on understanding and then managing the intersection of these three forces.

Globalization

Globalization has its supporters and detractors. From an economic standpoint and, in our opinion from a brand standpoint, "globalization is meant to signify integration and unity."[3] On the one hand, customers love the comfort of seeing familiar brands anywhere they travel. They appreciate the regularity and standardization. They are calmed by the familiarity and security that global brands provide. Perceiving a brand to be a global leader enhances the brand's stature. However, customers are concerned about the increasing homogeneity of the global marketplace. They fear what they see as the loss of authenticity and regional relevance. They are concerned about corporate domination. They believe that big, global enterprises jeopardize smaller local, "more authentic" entrepreneurial businesses. "Mass is becoming a problematic word in the global marketplace. Bespoke and crafted and boutique are good words."[4]

Globalization is real, and it is accelerating as the world becomes more interconnected. What happens anywhere can affect us everywhere. Financial markets are integrated globally. Political, social, and military events have international impact. Local environmental actions have global implications. Diseases that do not respect national boundaries have global implications. And information about all of these issues as well as any others travels around the world at lightning speed.

Localization

Localization has for some time been seen to be the antidote to globalization by providing that special sense of place. Locally sourced, locally crafted, locally owned, regionally authentic, one-of-a-kind, and so on bring a sense of cultural, ethnic, economic, and social connection that globalization cannot offer. Artisanal cheeses from a specific region, local distilleries and breweries, grass-fed cows on local farms, cage-free chickens, arts and crafts, non-GMO, fresh, organic, locally made employing local people, and other local elements and activities that bring "real" into our lives continue to grow and are increasingly attractive and affordable. U.S.-based Beringer Vineyards advertises that it keeps the starlings off its grapes by hiring a local falconer. They call it "Working with Nature. Working with Neighbors." And the advertising states that you can "Get local knowledge at beringer.com and facebook.com/beringervineyards."[5]

Yet, localization can become too forced, cute, involuntary, obligatory, and compulsory. It can go from creative to kitschy pretty quickly.

Marketers can go overboard in the desire to create an authentic local feeling. Las Vegas comes to mind. Why go to Venice when I can experience Venice with its canals, piazzas, gondolas, and gondoliers between the Venetian and the Palazzo hotels? With the access to widely available information, people easily figure out when an experience is over-the-top and the "designed" authenticity is false. Some of Tesco's recent problems globally are tied to its failure in attempting localization: selling live turtles and toads in the grocery did not seem to work for Tesco in China, forcing a sale of the majority of the business.[6]

Another side of localization is nationalism. This is creating tense political situations worldwide. Matthew Burrows calls it "a splintered world" in his book *The Future Declassified*. He looks at the diffusion of power, rising middle classes, rise of cities, intraregional trade, population shifts, porous borders, and countries that are emerging from developing to developed.[7] However, nationalism as an expression of local benefits and cultural uniqueness can help soften the homogeneity of a global brand.

The Economist calls this model of conditional, interventionist, and nationalistic behavior the "gated globe." The premise of the gated globe is that countries and companies have pushed the pause button on globalization.[8] From a brand standpoint, this is an oversimplification. Globalization has not stopped. It has been moderated by the collision of globalization with localization and personalization.

Localization is real, and we interact with it in a variety of ways. Think about the produce you can buy in your local grocery store. You can buy the limes from Mexico, or you can opt for something grown in the United States. People resist the threat of losing national and local identity. They want to protect local economies, values, and traditions. They appreciate the closeness and distinctiveness of their local world. They fear the perceived homogenization of the global village. They believe that "made locally" is worth protecting.

TOMS is a company with a mission. Millions of children around the world have no shoes to protect their feet. So TOMS promises to match every pair of shoes purchased with a pair of new shoes given to a child in need. The Holiday 2014 catalog for TOMS is called "Gift Local. Give Global." In other words, for every TOMS gift you buy for your family and friends in your local inner circles, you become a global giver of help for the needy. Behind the "Gift Local. Give Global." campaign is the concept that each gift you buy "has a unique way of giving back."[9]

The *Wall Street Journal* reported that a group in Minnesota is focusing on branding the state as "North" to create a region that will be known for more than a part of the U.S. Midwest. This young creative group thinks the Midwest is seen as more bland than bold. The idea is to enhance the "innovative, sturdy character of Minnesota honed by long cold winters." The group is using products that are made in Minnesota to make their point: Duluth Packs (backpacks, and so on), Frost River Bags, Sanborn Canoe, Red Wing Shoes, Faribault Wool Products, and North Hats.[10]

Personalization

Adding to globalization and localization is a third disruptive force: personalization. Personalization is growing in dimension and strength.

Personalization is real. Brands that create personalized experiences are valued. They promise to meet an individual's physical, psychological, social, and emotional needs. Personalization reinforces respect, status, and positive self-image.

Personalization is different from customization. We tend to use the words interchangeably; this is wrong. Customization focuses on features and functions—the practical aspects of a brand—readying the brand for a transaction. A custom-made Nike shoe is about finding the features you like—colors, stripes, laces, and so on—creating a transactional event. It is similar to finding your measurements and fabrics that customize a bespoke silk suit or shirt. Personalization is experiential. It happens when, based on who you are and what you like, an entire branded experience is created.

Personalization and Privacy

Effective data mining combined with flexible manufacturing and customized service delivery is facilitating superior personalization. However, there is a fine line between individual personalization and invasion of privacy. Many people are becoming uncomfortable with the degree to which brands, government, and media are using personal data. At some point, personalization becomes snooping, and then snooping becomes scary. Beyond just data, we live in a new world of constant surveillance through biometrics, transponders in our cars, and street-level and retail store video cameras or drones.[11]

Enormous amounts of data create a clear tension between personalization and privacy. The battle is just beginning. The conveniences of our digital, algorithmic world impose on our inherent sense of what is too personal or too private to share. People want to control with whom this information is shared. Predictive analytics is in the forefront of this argument. Anticipation of customer needs can also be perceived to be an invasion of customer privacy. We will address this topic again later in the book.

In the sharing economy, Uber, Lyft, RelayRides, ZipCar, and Airbnb are examples of brands that are managing at the intersection of globalization, localization, and personalization. They have created global presences that maintain certain standards while recognizing the needs of different local environments. They are finding that countries have different barriers to overcome, and those require different solutions. At the same time, each takes advantage of the new collaborative consumption on a local and personal basis for each user.

The marketing challenge is that these forces are not happening sequentially or independently. It is the simultaneous interaction and collision of these that is the challenge.

Implications for Organizational Structure

Just going global is not the same as being a global company. This is a lesson that LEGO recently learned, as described in *The Economist*.[12] A global company recognizes that being global means accepting localism and personalization.

The complexity of managing brands at the intersection of these three colliding forces requires changes to a company's organizational structure, including a changed mind-set. The old-fashioned, military model of command and control will no longer work; the local interests need to be expressed and leveraged, and the customer's personal interests need to be catered to and improved after each use. It is necessary to share responsibility for actions across geography and across functions. This will mean that some central functions cede responsibilities to the regions, whereas regional teams take on more responsibilities. This concept of shared responsibility is the driver of The Collaborative

Three-Box Model that we will discuss in detail further in this book. It is the flexibility of The Model that makes it so applicable for modern marketing. It is a method and mind-set that allows for mastery of these three forces.

For many brand organizations and the companies that own them, shifting the internal mind-set and introducing transparent collaboration are difficult to achieve. But if brands are going to be successful against the backdrop of globalization, localization, and personalization then, as difficult as it may be, it will be worth it. One of the critical factors for changes of this sort is leadership, not just at the top but throughout the entire enterprise.

Organized Leadership

A shared responsibility model necessitates organizing for leadership. To "organize" means to arrange interdependent parts into a structure designed for coordinated actions so everyone is working toward the same common goal. This becomes increasingly difficult when regional, local, and nationalistic forces come into play. Organizing means having close, tight coordination and laser-like focus. Everyone is asked to achieve time-dependent performance targets. Organizations with central, ensiled, order-giving functions will have to give up some of their responsibilities. Regional functions that behaved as order-takers will now have to implement and accept accountability for results. That can be accomplished, but it does take strong leadership from the top down.

How We Define Leadership

As we discuss in detail when we look at The Collaborative Three-Box Model, leadership is not the same as management. And, as we already pointed out, effective collaborative leadership is built on these five principles:

1. **Inspiration**—Defining a motivating vision and goals. What is the organizational ambition? Why should we care?

2. **Education**—Clarifying why this new vision is important. What will we have to do differently to succeed? How will we do it?

3. **Influence**—Impacting the work of others through guidance, experience, and expertise rather than relying only on direct command and control. The leader must be a collaborative authority bringing people together (unifying the teams) for productive action on behalf of the brand.

4. **Support**—Not just hoping that people will perform differently, but by providing the necessary training and tools. We provide tangible and emotional encouragement and reinforcement to help people resist the cultural tendencies to return to old habits.

5. **Evaluation**—Providing regular progress reports based on relevant metrics. We also mean recognizing and rewarding people who produce the right results the right way.

Columnist, writer, and thinker David Brooks wrote that the United States needs a "unifying leader" who Mr. Brooks describes is skilled in the art of collaboration. The collaborative leader is the one who "has rejected the heroic, solitary model of leadership. He doesn't try to dominate his organization as its all-seeing visionary."[13] We never would have experienced the remarkable turnaround results we did at McDonald's from 2003 to 2004 if it were not for the effective collaborative leadership of Jim Cantalupo and Charlie Bell.

Cross-Functional Teams (CFTs)

Cross-functional teams (CFTs) are an important way to achieve shared responsibility. Carlos Ghosn, as CEO of Nissan, determined during his first year that CFTs provide a reservoir of creative ideas while serving to break down structural and hierarchical barriers.[14] There is nothing more stifling than the organizational protectionism of powerful silos. As David Aaker points out, silos inhibit brand building. Many brand-building programs require global participation. Resource allocation requires functional and regional transparency. Global or wide-scale geographic communications require clarity and consistency. Silos impede these types of brand-building actions.[15]

Sharing across function and geography promotes organizational learning. Shared global learning generates new ideas and reduces redundancy in knowledge gathering. Companies in which functions or managers hoard data and knowledge slow the implementation of programs and progress.

Alignment

Collaboration needs alignment, which means creating adherents, not just acceptors. Buy-in is not good enough. This is not a poker game; you cannot take your cards and fold. As Ken Kesey (author of *One Flew Over the Cuckoo's Nest*, scholar, counterculture protagonist, and owner of the bus *Furthur*) said, "You're either on the bus or off the bus."[16] Organizations need to initiate changes regarding how people work together. This is an attitudinal issue as well as a structural one. People need to be on the bus or get off the bus.

Global, Local, and Personal Implications for Brand Management

The effects and consequences of this altering landscape are broad but can be handled. Here are five implications for managing brands due to globalization, localization, and personalization. These are actions that brands should implement now.

1. **Clarify the new roles of the global teams and the new roles of the regional teams**—What do I need to do? What is my job? What do I need to do differently? How will effectiveness be evaluated? Why is this job, my job, important? Where do I fit in the structure? What happened to make this job change necessary? People need to know what their job requires and what is not in their purview. People are interested in what is in it for them, so it is important not to overcomplicate the structure and the job descriptions. They need to know in no uncertain terms who does what and why. These definitions must be clear and precise. Lines of reporting must be obvious and explicit. Lack of clarity, including language and description, is a distraction at the very least and thoroughly confusing and unproductive. Everyone must speak the same language and use the same terminology.

2. **Generate a collaborative brand-focused culture**—Many organizations "walk the walk" on brand and even use the language of

brand, but there is really no buy-in. For example, a company may say that Brand Preference is its goal, yet there is no metric for Brand Preference. Where is the necessary information for understanding how things are going if there is no metric? Or a company will take the time in the annual report to talk about brand and its effect on the business but nothing in the business changes. Brand is a nice thing to mention, but it sometimes remains a meaningless construct. Brand building can still be seen as a cost for which marketers find it difficult to justify with measurable results.

3. **Stimulate and activate a return on global learning as an imperative**—We live in an information age, in which information is easily accessed online. Yet, there is an unfortunate information-based global corporate habit that negatively affects productivity: information hoarding. Information-hoarding behavior is wasteful and is an ineffective way to manage a business. From a resource allocation standpoint, keeping your data to yourself costs the company money, time, and effort. It also puts a drain on intellectual property because no one knows where a lot of the data and studies reside. At one client, a review of the job orders showed that more than 100 different projects worldwide were focusing on the very same initiative across geography with no cross-fertilization at all. It is really quite ironic that in a world we call the sharing economy, brand personnel sometimes resist sharing information with their colleagues, as if everyone is a competitor rather than a partner. This behavior is "brand defeating" and reason defying in today's highly competitive and volatile environment.

4. **Encourage regional and local creativity**—Somehow we often find ourselves in a corporate world in which innovation is led from the top down or the center outward. This is old-think conduct. Great ideas do not care where they come from. A powerful idea is not linked to a place or a position; it is linked to a purpose. Leadership means accepting ideas from anyplace and anyone. But leadership also means supporting the dissemination of these ideas and inspiring more creative people.

5. **Build internal pride in the brand function worldwide**—Marketing has become a trade rather than a profession. This shift has been self-inflicted. Marketing often falls in love with the tactics of the time. Today, it is the increasing variety of communication channel tactics: social media, entertainment, events, online, mobile, and so on. But communications channel management is not marketing management. The tactical splintering of functions is fracturing the role of marketing and changing the role of the CMO. It is difficult to generate internal, employee pride when marketing is sliced, diced, spliced, strangled, and mangled by specialists competing with each other for limited corporate resources. The CMO's role is often reduced to managing this competition and attempting to force co-operation. On the other hand, because there is a lack of serious measurement to demonstrate the financial benefits of the brand-building efforts, brand and marketing tend to be relegated to a functional level of activities rather than creating serious strategies.

Marketing is about managing the business, and managing the business is bigger than managing messages and media. From working with clients as internal and external consultants, we learned that effective marketing is not merely about message and media management; it is about business management. The business plans and the brand plans need to be integrated, not segregated.

Brand management is fundamentally about attracting more customers who purchase more often and become more loyal, generating more sales, and becoming more profitable. It is about generating value for customers and creating value for the company. To increase shareholder value, a brand must generate customer value. To build brand value, it is essential to manage the relationship between what customers are willing to pay in terms of their costs relative to the experience they receive for those cost expenditures.

The Role of the Three Forces

Globalization, localization, and personalization affect the ways in which global brands are managed. Over the years, as we will discuss, the approaches to global brand marketing have evolved. These three powerful forces shape the way organizations form around brands. They affect how companies hire for brands and define how companies market and manage their brands across geography.

This is different from the role of trends. Game-changing trends are ideas that change the way products and services are designed, renovated, changed, communicated, disseminated, and eliminated. Game-changing trends cause sparks for innovation. Game-changing trends affect the look and feel of brands.

Endnotes

1. Van Dyck, Paul and Johnston, Jan, "Kaleidoscope of Chaos," *Reflections*, Nde Music, 2003.

2. Pentland, Alex, *Social Physics: How Good Ideas Spread—The Lessons from a New Science*, The Penguin Press, NY, 2014, p. 3.

3. Rosenberg, Tina, "Globalization," *New York Times*, August 18, 2002.

4. Cohen, Roger, "Status in the New Asia," *New York Times*, Op-Ed, May 12, 2014.

5. See Beringer Vineyards ad page in *Wine Spectator*, December 31, 2014–January, 15, 2015, p. 34. This print campaign also runs in the *New Yorker* magazine.

6. Waldmeir, Patti, "China Headwinds Knock Tesco Partner," *Financial Times*, November 15–16, 2014.

7. Burrows, Matthew, *The Future Declassified*, Palgrave Macmillan, NY, 2014, pp. 43–64.

8. "The Gated Globe," a special report on the world economy, *The Economist*, October 12, 2014.

9. TOMS, Holiday 2014, TOMS.com, 2014.

10. Binkley, Christina, "Go North: Minnesota's New Cool," *Wall Street Journal*, January 22, 2015.

11. For an interesting discussion of surveillance and privacy, see Mack, Timothy C., "Privacy and the Surveillance Explosion," *The Futurist*, January–February 2014.

12. Schumpter, "Unpacking Lego: How the Danish Firm Became the World's Hottest Toy Company," *The Economist*, March 8, 2014.

13. Brooks, David, "The Unifying Leader," Op-Ed, *New York Times*, November 24, 2014.

14. Ghosn, Carlos and Rìes, Philippe, *Shift: Inside Nissan's Historic Revival*, Currency Doubleday, 2003, p. 106.

15. Aaker, David, *Aaker on Branding: 20 Principles That Drive Success*, Morgan James Publishing, NY, 2014, pp. 183–184.

16. Slattery, Maureen, ed., *Radical Times: Quotes from the Sixties*, Barnes & Noble Books, NY, 2004, p. 44.

3

Game-Changing Trends

The future has long lines
The future looks like a screen
It's all you'll ever see
All lit up like a stadium
Who will be the first?
The future has long lines
The future looks like a screen
And I cannot believe
The future's happening to me.

—Nada Surf[1]

Future-Proofing Your Brands

We cannot forecast the future with certainty, although we all want reliable forecasts of the future. People and organizations want certainty about tomorrow before making decisions today. Yet forecasting is fallible. As futurist Hugues de Jouvenal stated, "The objective is not to forecast the future, for no-one can tell what the future will be. The objective is to take responsibility as an organization for the future."[2] Being prepared for the future is called *future-proofing*; it is making sure that your brand or your organization is ready, agile, and able to accept, withstand, and make changes for enduring profitable growth. Future-proofing is not foolproof, but it is a serious step in the right direction.

Trends are current, existing developments affecting global societies. They are a hot topic among marketers, companies, financiers, sociologists, and futurists. However, trends are inherently backward facing because they are changes and events that are already happening. Trends are not the future, but they create a context for understanding what the future might be. Trends can provide actionable insights, but they are not actual forecasts. Helpful forecasts are based on a creative synthesis of insights from a variety of sources (including trends), actual observations, and experiences. It is about seeing what others fail to see. It is about pattern recognition when others see no pattern at all. It is about taking familiar information and putting it together in unfamiliar ways. Brands can be future-proofed by having insights into what is going on and what opportunities may be available.

Game-Changing Trends as Problems

Every speculation about trends begins with defining a "problem." We look at five trends as "problems" that brands and organizations can solve. For each of these problems, we will discuss potential "solutions" that brands and companies can use to design successful strategies.

How these problems play out and how brands leverage them will sort the winners from the losers. There is so much going on in the world that it would take an entire book just to describe all the potential developments and movements. The five trends we focus on have global implications covering developed and developing nations.

1. The Demographic Conundrum

Demographic researchers point out, "Of those people born in industrialized nations since 2000, more than 50% will live to be over 100 years old."[3] "The world is entering a demographic transformation of unprecedented dimensions."[4] Our world has become older and younger at the same time. And, regardless of which age you are, you will live longer. Longevity is affecting both ends of the age spectrum. The over-65-year-olds are living into their 80s and beyond. Younger people can expect to live well beyond 80 years old.

In 2012, 11.5% of the world population was over the age of 60 years old, and this group is expected to grow to 22% by 2050. Global life expectancy will rise from 69 years old in the five-year span, 2010–2015, to 76 years old by 2045–2050.[5] Many countries are already feeling the impacts on pensions, workforces, healthcare, politics, the military, and socioeconomic forces.

On the other hand, fewer women are having babies. In 2008, there were already "18 countries with contracting populations. By 2050, there will be 44, the vast majority of them in Europe. As historian Niall Ferguson has written, we are about to witness 'the greatest sustained reduction in European population since the Black Death of the fourteenth century.'"[6]

It used to be that the demographic charts had one big bulge: the Boomers (1946–1964). This bulge just moved up the age range as it matured. Now, with the addition of the Millennials (1982–2000), the demographic charts look like a two-humped camel—a two-humped camel that will be with us for decades.

Two massive age cohorts with different world views, different values, and different complexities pose an interesting conundrum for brands: which of these age groups should be targeted? What will a brand need to do differently? This is an interesting challenge not just in terms of product and service, but also in terms of communications, including package design. Font size is critically important. The weight of a box or a product is critically important. Age matters across all communications pathways.

Some companies have already chosen their strategic paths. The iconic U.S. retailer Macy's in New York City, home of the Macy's Thanksgiving Day Parade and the old film *Miracle on Thirty-Fourth Street*, has decided to focus on Millennials and tourists.[7] The News Corporation decided to attract Millennials who "do not have the reading habit" using an app designed just for them.[8]

The U.S. cable channel A&E decided to cancel a highly popular series called *Longmire* based on western stories by Craig Johnson. *Longmire* was one of A&E's most watched programs with an average of 5.6 million viewers per episode in 2013. The average age of the viewer, however, was 60 years old. A&E's rationale for the cancellation was that advertisers want to reach people under the age of 50. After the show's cancellation, the online uproar was extensive. That is when Netflix decided to pick up the series and stream it through its online service. Although the audience is still older, streaming on Netflix has created a new popularity among the Millennial generation. In fact, it's so popular that Netflix has ordered ten more episodes from *Longmire* creator, Warner Bros.[9]

Pizza Hut, the global pizza chain from YUM! Brands, changed its menu and its advertising to "alter perceptions assuring consumers, particularly members of the Millennial generation, that Pizza Hut understands how ardently they are embracing different foods and flavors."[10]

In contrast, the *Financial Times* ran a special series section called "Silver Economy" in its daily paper focusing on the economic issues of the aging "ageless" population of those 50 years old and older. (Demographically, with 1964 as the last year of Boomers, by 2015, all Boomers will be over 50 years old.)

Recognizing the strategic challenges of communicating to two different demographic groups, the *Financial Times* devoted a page to the dilemma faced by advertisers who have focused primarily on Millennials, pointing out that the "youth-dominated" advertising industry had better start understanding Boomers, who are estimated to have a global spending power of U.S. $15 trillion.[11] Boomers may be older, but they have the discretionary income to spend. They are also a more optimistic generation than Millennials. The concept of "silver design"—buildings designed for the aging population—is fast becoming a new area of "healthcare."[12]

The role of technology is a defining factor among the differences between Millennials and Boomers. If you are a Millennial, you grew up with a mobile phone and a computer. You learned to keep your parents at ease by letting them know where you are at every moment, even if you were not where you were expected to be. If you grew up as a Millennial, "gaming" did not mean sitting at a blackjack table in Las Vegas. You may have met your college roommate on Facebook. You may have had your college courses streamed online so you did not have to get out of bed to attend class. You researched your homework online. Your world view is of light-speed technological change. Hyper-connectivity does not make you hyper. You do not have to reach a comfort zone with technology; technology *is* your comfort zone.

Boomers do not have that same world view. Boomers were enchanted with the Princess phone design in the 1960s: a slim line lightweight oval of buttons with no rotary to dial! In their first jobs, they witnessed the change from IBM Selectrics to desktop computers with White-Out replaced by Word. They used Telefax machines to communicate internationally; they know what a mimeograph machine is and why you would use one. Entranced, Boomers watched as televisions ensconced in large wooden cabinets became household must-haves. For Millennials, mobile YouTube easily replaced gathering around the furniture that contained the TV tube. Now the TV screen, if it is watched (usually by their parents), is a wafer-slim, wall-mounted cinema-like element.

Both Boomers and Millennials see technology as positively affecting their lives. Both use technology and keep up with the advances. Boomers are certainly not technology Neanderthals. But they do retain a sense of marvel at the devices and the dimensions of technology, while Millennials expect new products and services to inspire their lives and help them make connections to expand their world.[13]

Yes, wars, terrorism, political upheavals, and economic shifts affect how Boomers see the world relative to Millennials. But these generational differences based on technology and its dispersion highlight how interesting strategic planning must become. The way you see the world changes the way you interact with people, services, and brands. For example, research presented in 2014 indicated that although both demographic cohorts will complain when there is a service break, Millennials are more likely to complain to a million people online compared to Boomers, who will first look for the person in charge and possibly complain to as many as 20 friends and family.[14]

The outcome of such a situation is clear: Boomers share their positive and negative experiences using traditional problem-resolution avenues, whereas Millennials are online sharing their experiences with vast numbers of people globally and instantaneously.

Another example affects the workforce. One of the findings of recent research indicates that, compared to Boomers, Millennials place more value on work that provides intrinsic and social rewards. It is one of the first quantitative studies to support the generational shift in work values. Overall, compared to Boomers, Millennials prefer not to work hard but still want status and money, creating a sense of entitlement. Millennials value leisure time.[15]

This study is supported by another recent survey of 16,000 Millennials from 43 countries. This new INSEAD research shows that Millennials are ambitious for the top jobs, but they want roles that have meaning and contribute to society. They also want to rise through the company on their own terms. The data show that 73% choose work-life balance over more money.[16] And interestingly, in Germany, because of this type of workplace trend, Boomers are being recruited to return to work because a shortage of younger staff is looming.[17]

Princess Cruises conducted a study in 2012 looking at Boomers and Millennials. The study indicated that the differences in travel habits are significant. Whereas one in three Boomers say they could not disconnect when on vacation, one in six Millennials say the same is true. A vacation get-away will not stop 85% of Millennials from making a social media update. In contrast, less than half of Boomers would update a social profile while on vacation."[18] These travel differences are supported by additional research such as the Boston Consulting Group's *Traveling with Millennials*.[19]

One of the most striking differences in world view between Millennials and Boomers is the Millennial mobile mind-set. For Millennials, mobile is not a channel. It is a way of thinking and behaving; it is an attitude and a belief. Millennials are much more connected than generations in the past, but for them "being connected" is more than "being in touch." Constant connection is an outlook and a given; it is a cosmic umbilical cord that creates a virtual safety net.

Forrester, the digital research company, stated that the mobile mind-set is the expectation that I can get what I want in my immediate context. Mobile redefines and expands what it means to meet people's needs; this situation was inconceivable before mobile phones. Most Boomers did not grow up expecting to have instant access to their desired—and needed—information and services using their fingers, 24/7, anywhere, anytime, immediately.[20]

Risk and investing are turning out to be differentiators as well. It used to be that people became more risk averse as they aged. But today's Boomers and even some of their living parents are taking greater risks in investments. A 2014 *Financial Times* online survey of 4,200 readers indicated that 27% of over-60 respondents would weight their portfolios toward stocks.[21] Meanwhile, the *Wall Street Journal* pointed out that the Millennial generation fears stocks. Citing a 2013 study by Wells Fargo, the article says that 52% of Millennials are "not confident" or "not at all confident" in the stock market. Why? Partly because a Millennial who was born in 1980, and would have invested $100, would have made just $1030 when he or she turned 30 years old. Contrast this with someone born in 1970 who invested $1000 and now has $5400.[22]

Another aspect of technology and the mobile mind-set is speed. The ability to access what you want instantly changes the way you live your life. It shortens the decision-making process. (We will discuss this in a later chapter.) We live in a world where "now" is the operative word.

Boomers do embrace technology and do own mobile phones. Many of them can even afford to keep up with the latest models. But Boomers, in general, relate to the mobile phone inherently as a mobile phone. Millennials feel differently. Millennials are quite comfortable with the concept that this is much more than a phone. It is a portable informational and relational appliance that is mobile and instant.

This conundrum of marketing to Millennials compared to marketing to Boomers has many dimensions, some of which we have just described. The differences between these two demographic cohorts affect all industries. It is an underlying theme in the next problem to be solved: the rise of personalization.

2. The Challenges of Rising Personalization

Personalization affects the way the teams are organized and hired. It affects the delivery of the product and service at point of sale, wherever that may be. But it also affects brand renovation and innovation. Personalization seems to be touching all aspects of managing, marketing, and designing brands. Its growth is startling.

As we discussed in the previous chapter, our world is more interconnected across geography. People are increasingly appreciating their local relevance and their personal differences. Marketing is becoming more customized, more individualized, and more personalized. Those local differences, cultural differences, and personal differences are not vestiges of the past but the vision of the future, and that future is already here.

People appreciate the value of products and services designed to satisfy individual needs and create individualized, exceptional branded experiences. Personalization delivers a respectful recognition of who I am as a person by reflecting back to me and to others aspects of my personality. Personalization satisfies my needs and problems in ways that might not work for someone else.

To receive a personalized experience, people are willing to provide brands and organizations with vast quantities of intimate behavioral data. Technology and the multiple types of devices now available have paved the way for this extraordinary ability to personalize just about any request.

Personalization generates a unique form of brand engagement. It is a virtuous cycle if handled properly. The more the customer likes the experience and trusts the source, the more information she is likely to provide; the more information provided, the more personalized; and so forth. This virtuous circle of "experience personalization" that is targeted to a specific individual can "give rise to a version of customer loyalty akin to religious devotion greater than brand affinity."[23]

Additionally, personalization can happen immediately, in real time, enhancing the desire for immediate satisfaction. This fuels our impulse inferno. Technology can be attuned to the user's needs, anticipating behavior, and then, instantly satisfying future needs with a recommended song, a curated news site, selected sports scores, a recommended variety of entertainment options, and so on.

Permissible Personalization

As we pointed out, there is always that fine line between personalization and prying. Recently, the *New York Times* Op-Ed page featured a piece on *predictive shopping*. Predictive shopping is when the brand or company determines what you might want to buy prior to your even knowing you might choose this item. The article highlighted the pros and cons of predictive shopping and stated that customers are okay with predictive shopping for "basics" such as paper towels and dish soap. Customers were negative about predictions for things that they did not yet realize they wanted or needed.[24]

This idea—that predictive marketing has its limits—is supported by other research-based discussions we have been involved in showing that customers see a difference between prediction and remembering. Remembering is based on recollection and memory. If you remember me based on previous experiences with me, it is as if I made an impression on you. We call this *Permissible Personalization*. Remembering my name and preferences based on my past behaviors with a particular brand shows respect and recognition. Predicting what I might want for lunch based on external data such as my Facebook information or other "big data" sources is sometimes viewed as creepy and unwanted.

Brands and organizations have to personalize. But it will be in everyone's best interests if we respect the limitations—when personalization crosses the privacy border. Millennials appear to have more porous lines between personal and private because they have been avid sharers for most of their lifetime. However, we now know that the Edward Snowden case strongly affected Millennials in deeper ways than expected when it comes to government surveillance "snooping."[25] U.S. TV procedural dramas such as *CSI, NCIS, Law & Order,* and *Criminal Minds* show how quickly and easily law enforcement and criminals can access personal information.

Additionally, brands need to determine what kinds of personalization are best suited for the brand. This is common sense. For example, if you are a fast food restaurant and must deliver the order in 60 seconds, offering personalized meals that take 3–4 minutes may not be the road to riches. In fact, it may turn away customers who do not want to wait. In this case, personalization needs to fit into the brand parameter of "fast."

The rise of personalization underscores the desire for a focus on "me" in ways that the Me generation could hardly match. Yet, at the same time, we are becoming an increasing networked and sharing economy. The importance of these two paradoxical desires, "me and we," shape the third problem facing brands and organizations: The paradox of the Age of I.

3. The Paradox of the Age of I

Personalization of customer experiences is a growing customer expectation based on our accelerating desires for individualized experiences reflecting personal needs, attitudes, and situations. Customers want to be respected as individuals, but they also want to feel they belong to something bigger than themselves; they want the feeling of independence and interdependence at the same time (see Figure 3.1). "I am he as you are he and we are all together."[26] We call this a need for "inclusive individuality"—the theme of the Age of I. This is represented in the new Android campaign that states, "Be together. Not the same."[27]

Figure 3.1 Age of "I"

The explosion of digital and mobile allows marketers to cater to the need for "inclusive individuality." We have the ability to personalize and predict hyper-relevant experiences. Customers can individualize these experiences and share them with various global, regional, and local "communities" to which they choose to belong.

Today's focus on increased personalization is not the same as it was in the consciousness-raising, self-focused, self-absorbed, self-actualizing era of the 1960s and 1970s. Then, it was "all about me." "Let me do my own thing." "What's in it for me?" It was also a self-centered, self-interested, self-obsessed marketing era. We hailed nonconformity, broke with the past, welcomed anything antiestablishment, and rejected family values and structure.

Advertising during the "Age of Me" reflected this "me-mentality." Now defunct Braniff Airlines ran an ad featuring Andy Warhol and Sonny Liston using Liston's mantra: "If you got it, flaunt it." Nice 'N Easy Hair Color said, "It lets me be me." Hertz said, "Hertz puts you in the driver's seat."

Historian Richard Miller wrote, "(the 60s)...was about liberty, meaning the absence of physical, mental, emotional, cultural, and even biological restraint.... This idea...is Autonomy."[28]

Today's new age of "Inclusive Individuality" is different. We have the intersection of individuality with the simultaneous desire for inclusiveness. Instead of the world revolving around us, we want a world that understands, respects, and recognizes us. True, we savor individuality, but we desire inclusivity at the same time. We want to be independent yet interconnected. Our individual commonalities are important. We want to be unique, and we want to share our uniqueness with like-minded people.

Digital connections make all this possible. We are independent individuals who belong to multiple, virtual communities. We have gone from *Self Magazine* to selfies. We have left counterculture for the connected culture.

Modern marketing requires that we adopt an approach that informs and maximizes both individuality and inclusiveness. Consumers want a constant, continuing flow of valuable, relevant, and engaging experiences, either in person or virtually delivered via articles, blog posts, live events, videos, photos, positive reinforcement, sounds, sales, and social media. They want to respond as individuals, and they want to share as members of a community of common interests. "I am an individual with unique individual wants and needs. But I am not alone. I belong to local/regional/global communities of people who want the same things as I do."

This digital, sharing mobile mind-set is great news for brands. Digital allows content to be rich and engaging. As David Aaker states in *Aaker on Branding*, "An engaged audience will be susceptible to listening, learning, believing and behavior change...."[29]

Retirees in the United States are creating their own communities called Virtual Villages. All that is required is a yearly fee, and they gain access to resources and social connections. Older people can now stay at home and still be networked, can find services they need, and can call their own shots.[30] They keep and enhance their individuality while gaining the benefits of belonging.

The Inclusive Individualist is a marketing tsunami. This desire for maximizing both inclusivity and individuality at the same time encouraged through massive shifts in technology is affecting the very nature of our core relational bonds, changing the definition of family.

4. The Puzzling Changes in the Definition of Family

Brands and organizations will need to manage in a world where the basic values that underpin relationships are quickly altering. This is evident when it comes to the definition of family. The desires for both individuality and inclusivity, the new sharing nature of our economy, the aging of the population, multigenerational travel, and the "sole-ness" of many virtual experiences now emphasizes two distinct yet related concepts of what a family is.

Over the past few decades, the structure of families has undergone several iterations. The composition of the average 1950s "traditional family"—stable unit of mom, dad, two kids—has changed significantly with the rapid changes in the definitions of "family" arrangements such as these:

- Traditional family
- Single households
- Single-parent households
- Unmarried couples with or without children
- Same sex couples with or without children
- Multigenerational households
- Merged family households
- Adult living facility
- Sororities, fraternities, dormitories
- Transgender families
- Empty nesters
- Group living

Already in 1990, *The Futurist* commented, "More individuals will experience a greater variety of family situations over a lifetime."[31]

The family compositions detailed in the preceding list reflect the combinations and permutations of our kin family: those with whom we are bonded either by blood or through some "arrangement" such as adoption or marriage. Although divorce and remarriage are more prevalent and accepted today, kin families (if not born into one) take a while to adapt to and are hard to opt out of. The lines of "belonging" are less flexible. For example, as acrimonious as many divorces can be, parents often wind up "sharing" their children with each other on alternating weekends and holidays.

Kin families tend to define "my personal" life and generate mind-sets of "family first" or "leave my family out of this." The prestigious St. Regis hotel chain is communicating the idea that kin families create "memories" and "traditions" so you and your family should return time after time. The campaign simply says, "Family Traditions at St. Regis."[32] Disney has a special vacation promotion it calls "Magic Your Way" vacations packages; you can experience the flexibility of creating a vacation that fits your family's preferences, size, and budget.[33]

Along with our kin families, we have kindred spirit families. Our increased connectedness; our networked, sharing economy; our social sites such as Facebook, Twitter, and LinkedIn; and our online communities of shared interests such as Etsy, TripAdvisor, and Yelp all create a web of possibilities for families of kindred spirits. Kindred spirits families are online, digital, virtual, or physical "like-minded others" communities based on shared interests and values. Alex Pentland of MIT calls these "kith" relationships, as in "kith and kin." He points out that kith derives from Old English and Old German as a word for knowledge. Kith, then, "refers to a more or less cohesive group with common beliefs and customs." It is about a collective intelligence that flows from the group as a whole: "a group with shared, integrated habits and beliefs."[34]

The boundaries of "kith" or kindred spirits families are porous and flexible. You can opt in and opt out at will and belong to many at one time. There are no time limits to belonging; you can take as much time or as little time as you like. You may even express a different personality depending on the group or the cause or the strength of the particular interest.

Kin and kindred spirits families represent two different networks of relationships. They emphasize two different parts of who we are: the utmost in personalization. Kin and kindred spirits families reflect the paradox of the Age of I because these two family networks reinforce the desire to be both an individual and an inclusive member at the same time. Brands and the companies that own them will need to be cognizant of both types of families and create outreach for both.

For example, in an interview with Hugo Barra, the global vice president of the Chinese phone company Xiaomi, Mr. Barra stated that contrary to the interviewer's question as to the cult-like connections of the brand, Xiaomi is more like family. "Our core belief is that if you treat your customers as friends, if you listen to them carefully for their feedback, if you respect their views, if you really take care of them, they become attached to you and to your products. They tell their friends. They forgive your mistakes. They help you. It is kind of like becoming part of a family."[35]

For Millennials, the content generated in their kindred spirit families is more trusted than that generated by brands or experts. In fact, Millennials trust information found in user-generated content 50% more than information from traditional media sources. And user-generated content is 20% more influential than professional reviews when it comes to purchasing.[36] Becoming a trusted source is no small task in a world where trust is declining. This brings us to the fifth problem facing brands and companies today: the decline in trust.

5. The Quandary of the Decline of Trust

Trust in institutions is in decline all over the world. Each year, Edelman releases its Trust Barometer, and each year the news is slightly worse. As the 2014 issue of the report stated on its opening page,

> "The 2014 Edelman Trust Barometer shows the largest ever gap between trust in business and government since we began this study in 2001.... In nearly half of the 27 nations we surveyed, there is a gap of more than 20 points. In a few nations, the divide is as much as 40 points. This is a profound evolution in the landscape of trust from 2009, when business had to partner

with the government to regain trust, to today, when business must lead the debate for change."[37]

This situation that Edelman depicts is supported by the recent (September 2014) CNBC/Burson-Marstteller Corporate Perception Indicator study. This global survey of 25,000 general public respondents and 1,800 top executives from 25 markets indicates that trust in corporations is low. Although there are differences in perceptions regarding corporations between developed and developing countries, the overarching conclusion is the same: we face a world of ever-declining institutional trust.[38] Additionally, a survey of 114,000 people, this year's *Global Corruption Barometer* covering 107 countries indicated, "Less than 10% of people in the European countries hardest hit by the region's debt crisis say their leaders are doing a good job fighting corruption. Only 23% of those surveyed internationally believed that their government's efforts to fight corruption were effective, down from 32% in 2008.[39]

Trust is at the heart of every relationship. Every brand relationship has within it an element of trust. We define trust as the firm and confident belief in the reliability, truth, credibility, ability, or strength of someone or something. For brands and corporations, this means consistently delivering on promises. People want their products and services, and the representatives of these products and services, to be trustworthy. For a relationship of enduring brand loyalty to exist, trust must exist. People are more loyal to brands they trust.

And, as our world becomes more complex and uncertain, trust is a must. Brand and corporate trustworthiness is especially relevant and compelling in a volatile, changeable, uncertain world. Technology and ubiquitous information make customers more knowledgeable, demanding, value and quality conscious, smarter, conscientious shoppers. At the same time, customers are increasingly more skeptical, more questioning, and more uncertain.

When things are uncertain, people look for touchstones of trust. Trust is comforting and minimizes perceived risk. It is a relationship criterion more than a transaction criterion. It facilitates persuasion and the acceptance of new information. Trust affects the customer-perceived value of a brand. For example, people are more willing to accept a line extension from a brand they trust.[40]

Trust cannot be bought; it must be earned. Even though we live in an instant culture, trust cannot be earned instantly. It accumulates slowly and is earned over time. Trust is durable yet fragile. It is lasting, but when it is damaged, the bond can break quickly. It can take years to build and can be lost overnight.

The *Wall Street Journal* is currently using trust as its key message in its advertising. The headline of the *Journal*'s print campaign is, "Trust is something you earn." Viator.com, a travel guide website, ran a campaign in June 2014 stating, "Our guides are trustworthy."[41]

Millennials are especially skeptical when it comes to trust. As we pointed out earlier, they prefer to trust user-generated content rather than brands or professionals. Some Ipsos/Crowdtap research indicated that, "Millennials spend 18 hours a day consuming different media across several devices. User-generated content makes up 30% of that time (5.4 hours), second only to traditional media like print, television and radio at 33%." Not only do Millennials trust user-generated content, the study showed that user-generated content was 35% more memorable than other sources.[42]

Additionally, Lippincott, the corporate identity firm, created a white paper discussing the trust decline. The firm noted that since the mid-1970s, there has been a "precipitous decline in the trust of companies, from 34% to less than 20%. Loss of trust is even more noticeable in the under-35-year-old (Millennial) generation that is significantly less likely to trust companies."[43] Generating, building, nurturing, and continually growing trust is critical for brands, especially global and corporate brands that reach across geography.

Trends and the Forces of Globalization, Localization, and Personalization

It is hard to delineate whether 1) the three powerful forces of globalization, localization, and personalization are the context within which the game-changing trends evolve and morph, or 2) the game-changing trends create an environment that spurs on the three forces. Which comes first? All of these moving ideas exist. We can point to all the changes that are happening around us. We can see—and feel—how these changes affect our relationships. It is possible that the forces and the game-changers are two different sets of the same things. Or, some may argue that these are too different to put into the same bucket. However, as we ended the previous chapter, we said that the forces of globalization, localization, and personalization affect marketing in different ways.

The three forces have been and continue to be the underlying concepts driving how we manage brands across geography. The game-changing trends affect how products and services are defined or changed, innovated, or renovated.

Opportunities

We discussed the five game-changing, trending problems that brands and organizations face. These already exist, but they continue to morph and loom larger each year. All these problems are related to each other. Solving for one provides insights into solving for another. For each one, we identified some potential marketing opportunities that may lead you toward marketing solutions.

1. The demographic conundrum

2. The challenge of rising personalization

3. The paradox of the Age of I

4. The puzzling changes in the definition of family

5. The quandary of the decline in trust

1. Opportunity: Demography

Demography is a given, but it is not necessarily destiny. From a strategic standpoint, the successful brands will be those that can address both the Boomers and the Millennials. This is not an easy task. It requires strategic creativity. It means finding a focus for each of these two demographics against which your brand can deliver. Mass marketing is gone. The diverse types of media available and the way in which information can be displayed across media allow the marketer to speak to more than one group. Bring all disciplines to the table. Areas that you might feel are too tactical may have significant strategic importance, such as room design, package design, menu design, flavors, safety, and so forth.

As we discuss later in detail, the new marketing tool of Brand Journalism is perfect for this multiaudience situation. It allows a marketer to speak with different demographic groups while staying true to the essence of the brand. Brand Journalism as a marketing tool allows a brand to communicate across various media (including packaging, mobile, outdoor, online, and so on) to different audiences with different needs and values in different places and situations.

2. Opportunity: Personalization

Brand Journalism is also a flexible way to address some of the issues of personalization. Personalization is not just about targeted content; it is about delivering personalized experiences. This personalized content can be delivered virtually or in a real brick-and-mortar building, with real people doing the personalizing.

Millennials and Boomers will want different experiences from the same brand, each experience personalized for their own special needs and expectations. In the hospitality industry, for example, this means a focus on HR and hiring: hiring the personable person rather than training this characteristic. This is a huge task. It is much more than the sign outside a local West Palm Beach, Florida, McDonald's that says, "We're now hiring friendly people."

Finding the correct strategies to satisfy the needs of these two different cohorts takes diligence. It is not the same as offering a discount for senior citizens as the cinemas in the United States have been doing for years. Recognize that Boomers have different technological comfort zones than Millennials. Understand how these two groups feel about family and connectedness. Figure out the service need differences. These are areas for in-depth investigation and true insight.

3. Opportunity: The Age of I

The paradox of the Age of I continues to grow, as increasingly we want to stand apart from everything yet wish to be a part of something: "I want to be different just like all my friends." Personalization enhances both the individuality of the person and the inclusivity of the communities.

So, for example, travelers can use deeper elements of online travel sites using demographics to find "their tribe" and design a vacation or business trip suited just for their personal needs.[44] Apps that help us find the $5 cocktail happy hour or the gluten-free restaurant help us connect with people who have the same needs.[45] And, of course, there is Harley Davidson, where the biker tribesmen and woman happily tattoo the Harley Davidson logo on their bodies.

The ultimate in "tribe" behavior is what Bill Bishop describes as "urban sorting." Certain cities in the United States have become cultural urban centers for similarities in lifestyle and approach to life and politics. Portland, Oregon, is one that immediately comes to mind. However, Orange County, California; Brooklyn, New York; Palm Beach, Florida; Austin, Texas; and Houston, Texas, are other places where you can find like-minded others who want the same things, have the same politics, and favor the same food and cultural diversity or lack of it.[46]

Paul Roberts described this desire to be with people just like us—our kindred spirits—in this way:

> "More and more of our personal consumption is aimed at finding or creating "enclaves" of self-reflecting utility—places, products, experiences, networks, and people that reinforce our self-image and aspirations by emphasizing what we like and filtering out what we don't. For some of us, this process of personalization might mean a new neighborhood with just the right mix of prewar Craftsman bungalows and recycling bins. For others, it might be a group of online friends whose likes and dislikes mirror our own. It could be a political movement that confirms our deepest hunches about humanity.... It might be a brand."[47]

Leveraging the "sorting" behaviors can provide a new way to bring your brand to life. Outdoor media can address different "communities" of people through tailoring media by micro-locales. Aligning with and enhancing different communities of people has potential. At the same time, the Android approach of speaking to the paradox, tackling it head on, has a great deal of merit. Focus on the paradox promise: maximizing the benefits of two paradoxical needs. In its 1980s heyday, The Gap was a place where you could find things to wear to express your inner self while wearing what everyone else was wearing. J Crew has that panache today. The Army focuses on how you can be a better you while joining an organized "community." Buying that book you really love makes you feel special and different, but Amazon will tell you what others "like you" bought after buying that same book. Finding ways to satisfy the paradox promise can be a major, branded strategic opportunity.

4. Opportunity: Families

Looking deeper into the development of "communities," we can separate the families of kindred spirits from the original families from which we come and to whom we are connected throughout most of our lives. People today tend to belong to many more "families" that are not kin based. If we view these two sets of families as networks, it benefits brand and companies to leverage both sets of networks for each targeted individual. Thinking about all the "friends" people have today; focusing on a person's familial networks is like buying lists that used to be for the mail order business. Marketers should also consider "events" that bring in "families" of like-minded people. The Seattle Science Museum has a New Year's event that mixes science shows with a New Year's Eve party. It draws groups of like-minded people who then have the chance to see what learning the museum can provide in the context of a great gala event. In the 1970s, Dr. Pepper enticed consumers with the idea of "community" by asking people to "Be a Pepper." Coca-Cola urged people to get together (now) and be part of a global community with its "I'd like to teach the world to sing in perfect harmony" campaign.

5. Opportunity: Trust

Families of kin and kindred spirits are based on trust. People—especially those who are younger—have replaced trust in institutions with trust in communities of peers and like-minded others. Understand the needs and concerns of demographic cohorts with the rise of personalization within the changing context of the Age of I, and the ramifications these are having on the basic structures of relationships such as family, brands, and organizations to create significant actions that will build trust.

This is not an overnight fix: trust must be earned. But trustworthy behavior can be signaled through trustworthy actions, most specifically around sustainability and care for communities and the planet. Chipotle does this with Food with Integrity. Starbuck's does this with its continuing focus on Earth Day and other compassionate outreach programs. Toyota does this through its Prius brand.

The five Game-Changing Trends will continue for a long time. Each one has some connection to the other. Each creates a rich area for imagination, idea generation, innovation, renovation, and strategic and tactical alterations. These are addressable challenges for which there are already relevant actions.

However, this requires organizational will, openness, consistency of thought process, and language that underpins the idea of cross-functional, cross-geographic teamwork, which is at the core of The Collaborative Three-Box Model.

These problems facing brands have solutions. And there will be new solutions each year. These five components of our changing world set the context within which the three forces of globalization, localization, and personalization are colliding. The Collaborative Three-Box Model has a design that adapts itself to a forcefully fluctuating global environment.

Endnotes

1. Caws, Matthew, Lorca, Daniel, and Elliot, Ira, "The Future," *The Stars Are Indifferent to Astronomy*, Nada Surf, Barsuk Records, 2012.

2. De Jouvenals, Hugues, Futuribles, nonprofit center for prospective studies and foresight, France.

3. *Global Trend Report: Work, An Exploration of the Trends Shaping the Future of Work*, FutureNous 2012 in association with Shaping Tomorrow, 2013; citation from University of Southern Denmark, 2013.

4. Jackson, Richard and Howe, Neil with Rebecca Strauss and Keisuke Nakashima, "The Graying of the Great Powers: Demography and Geopolitics in the 21st Century," *Center for Strategic International Studies*, May 2008.

5. "Global Monitor: Macrodynamics," The Futures Company, 2013.

6. Jackson, Richard and Howe, Neil with Rebecca Strauss and Keisuke Nakashima, "The Graying of the Great Powers: Demography and Geopolitics in the 21st Century," *Center for Strategic International Studies*, May 2008. Also see Ferguson, Niall, "Eurabia?" *New York Times Magazine*, April 4, 2004.

7. Singer, Natasha, "Makeover on 34th Street," *New York Times*, Sunday Business Section, November 2, 2014.

8. Garrahan, Matthew, "New Corp Revisits the News App as It Targets 'Millennial' Readers," *Wall Street Journal*, July 13, 2014.

9. Flint, Joe, "Netflix Resurrects 'Longmire' Series," *Wall Street Journal*, November 20, 2014.

10. Elliott, Stuart, "In Overhaul, Pizza Hut Tries Adventurous Menu Offerings and a Dash of Irreverence," *New York Times*, November 19, 2014.

11. "Advertising's Aging Dilemma," *Financial Times*, Thursday, October 30, 2014. Estimated global spending quoted from *Euromonitor*.

12. Aronson, Louise, "New Buildings for Old People," *New York Times*, Opinion, November 2, 2014.

13. "The Rise of Generation C: Implications for the World of 2020," Booz Allen and Co., 2010; and "Introducing Generation C: The Connected Collective Consumer," Nielsen, October 2010.

14. IntelliResponse Survey, *Quirks Marketing Research Review*, July 2014.

15. Twenge, Jean M., Campbell, Stacy M., Hoffman, Brian J., Lance, Charles E., "Generational Differences in Work Value: Leisure and Extrinsic Values Increasing, Social and Intrinsic Values Decreasing," *Journal of Management*, March 10, 2010, Vol. XX, No. X.

16. De Vita, Emma, "Tips on Staff Productivity from a Happiness Evangelist," *Financial Times*, November 24, 2014.

17. Bryant, Chris, "German Economy Turns to Pensioner Power," *Financial Times*, September 2, 2014.

18. *The Princess Cruises 2012 Relaxation Report*, June 28–July 5, 2012, PR Newswire, August 7, 2012.

19. *Traveling with Millennials*, Boston Consulting Groups 2013, Bulldog Reporter's Daily Dog, March 29, 2013.

20. Benoff, Josh, Ask, Julie A., Schadler, Ted, Rogowski, Ron, "Mobile Moments Transform Customer Experience," Forrester, 2014.

21. Pickford, James, "Silver Generation Embraces Equity Risk," *Financial Times*, November 8–9, 2014.

22. Housel, Morgan, "A Letter to Younger Investors," *Wall Street Journal*, November 22–23, 2014.

23. Dalton, John, Sizemore, Amelia with Harley Manning and Curt Nichols, "Key Takeaways from Forrester's 2013 Customer Experience and Culture Forum," Forrester, 2013.

24. Sunstein, Cass, "Shopping Made Psychic, *New York Times*, Op-Ed, August 20, 2014.

25. Miller, Claire Cain, "Americans Say They Want Privacy, but Act as if They Don't," *New York Times*, November 13, 2014.

26. Lennon, Johan and McCartney, Paul, "I Am the Walrus," *Magical Mystery Tour*, Apple Records, 1967.

27. See a print, two-page, four-color spread for Android in the *New York Times*, October 16, 2014.

28. Miller, Richard, Bohemia: *The Protoculture Then and Now*, Nelson-Hall, December 1977.

29. Aaker, David, *Aaker on Branding: 20 Principles That Drive Success*, Morgan James Publishing, July 2014.

30. Gustke, Constance, "Retirees Turn to Virtual Villages for Mutual Support," *New York Times*, November 29, 2014.

31. *The Futurist*, September 1990.

32. See print ad in "How to Spend It" *Financial Times* magazine, November 1–2, 2014.

33. Disneyworld.disney.go.com/vacation-packages/2014/base.

34. Pentland, Alex, *Social Physics: How Good Ideas Spread—The Lessons from a New Science,*" The Penguin Press, NY, 2014, pp. 60–61.

35. Blumenthal, Rebecca, "No Stores. No Ads. Just a Lot of Sales," *Wall Street Journal,* November 3, 2014.

36. Knoblauch, Max, "Millennials Trust User-Generated Content 50% More Than Other Media," *Mashable.com,* April 9, 2014; reporting on a study by Ipsos and Crowdtap.

37. 2014 Edelman Trust Barometer, Edelman Berland.

38. Baer, Donald A., "The West's Bruised Confidence in Capitalism," *The Wall Street Journal,* September 22, 2014.

39. Eddy, Melissa, "Crisis-Struck Europeans Say They're Losing Faith in Governments," *New York Times International,* July 10, 2014.

40. Light, Larry, "Trust Is a Must," *Advertiser,* ANA, 2004.

41. See the *New York Times,* viator.com print ad, June 8, 2014.

42. Greenberg, Allen, "Millennials Trust People Over Brands," BenefitsPro, April 2014.

43. Lippincott, "Corporate Brand Discussion," June 2013.

44. Rosenbloom, Stephanie, "Finding Your Travel Tribe," *New York Times,* October 5, 2014.

45. Miller, Bryan, "The Touch Screen That Came to Dinner," *Wall Street Journal,* October 26–27, 2014, section D.

46. Bishop, Bill, *The Big Sort: Why the Clustering of Like-Minded Americans Is Tearing Us Apart,* Houghton Mifflin, Boston, MA, 2008. And, Roberts, Paul, *The Impulse Society: America in the Age of Instant Gratification,* Bloomsbury, NY, 2014, pp. 116–117.

47. Roberts, Paul, *The Impulse Society: America in the Age of Instant Gratification,* Bloomsbury, NY, 2014, p. 117.

4

New Definition of Brand Value: Trustworthy Brand Value

You say that time is money and money is time
So you got mind in your money and money on your mind

—Black Eyed Peas[1]

With all the changes happening around us, the concept of value remains important. Value is still a critical component of decision-making and a sought-after ideal. However, now it has a new definition.

What Is Value?

With the rapidly shifting world in which we live and do business and with all the forces that are appearing to intersect and collide, customer perception of brand value has changed. In its most basic definition, value refers to "what you get for what you pay." What you get is often defined as "the features and functions you get for the money you pay." The common definition of value is the price or cost of something. But value is far more than mere price. In business and especially in marketing, the definition of value is vague and ill-defined because there are so many differing definitions.

Over time, value assessment or the way people evaluate a brand's worth has evolved. A customer considers many aspects when assessing a brand's worth. People do not just think about price. When considering a brand's worth, people have a multidimensional value map in their minds. As Professors Tybout and Sternthal point out when speaking of value:

"This proposition is a conceptual definition rather than a mathematical one and serves as a tool for making comparisons. Managers may examine the value proposition of brands that compete for similar consumers or may explore a particular brand's proposition across segments, either at a point in time or over time."[2]

Value is a vague term in business and marketing because it has become a buzzword for *low price*. Marketers express this by pointing out, "This is our value brand." In fast food, value menus are small sizes for small prices; think of the Value Menu at Wendy's or the Dollar Menu at McDonald's. In December 2014, the *New York Times* wrote that McDonald's "...was reducing the number of "value" meals promotions of groups of items that together cost less than ordering items individually. It also tweaked its dollar menu, raising the price of many items to more than a dollar."[3] Tactics like these confuse the meaning of value by equating it with price.

Another outcome of this thinking is that value becomes associated with *deals*. To increase perceived value, marketers turn to increased emphasis on deals. "My hotel loyalty program has some great deals where I do not have to pay for breakfast and I get a free night," is an example of trying to increase value perception by focusing on the deal. This sorry turn of events is confusing and misleading.

Value Is Customer Defined

Value is not decided in a conference room. Marketers do not determine it; the customer does. Although marketers believe they are value creators, in fact, they help create brands to which customers ascribe value. Marketers determine pricing but not value. Price is a piece of the customer's value equation. But it is not the whole equation. Consumers decide whether the price marketers ask is fair for the experience they will receive. Instead of deciding *what to charge*, marketers should determine if the price they want to ask would be *a customer-perceived fair price*.[4] Marketers should evaluate whether the charged price is a fair value compared to the experience promised and delivered. Marketers must aim their brand to be the best value at whichever price point they place its offer. This approach treats pricing as a strategy, not a selling tactic. (As we describe later, pricing strategy is so important that your brand's pricing policy must be part of its Brand Framework.) Relative to competition, is your brand above, below, or inside the fair value corridor (see Figure 4.1)? Above the fair value corridor means the brand is perceived to be too high priced for the promised brand experience. As Professor George Day stated:

> "A winning position for customers is superior benefits for an average price. Most businesses position their offerings on the diagonal from the economy to the premium end and thus price their products to capture the customer value they created. However, some of the competitors will be off the diagonal, by accident or design. Those charging average prices for lower benefits are offering inferior value. Below the diagonal is superior value. Above the diagonal is inferior value."[5]

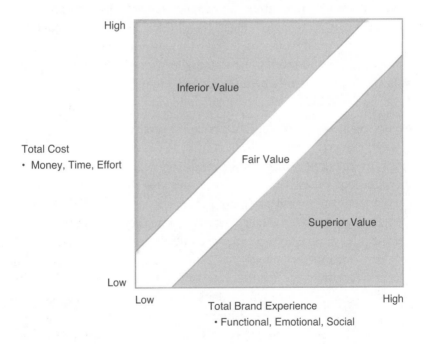

Figure 4.1 Fair value corridor

Price Segmentation

Looking only at money, marketers make the mistake of viewing their categories in terms of price segmentation. Price segmentation is a marketer's commonplace view of the competitive landscape. It is easy to do and easy to explain. Just carve up the marketplace by price point. Sometime the price points are given names such as mid-market, up-market, and premium. The automotive industry is great at this: entry-level, mid-luxury, near-luxury, luxury, premium. *Automotive News* had a story on the new Jaguar-Land Rover set of vehicles in November 2014. The group sales manager said, "...growth will come from two vehicle families—midrange luxury and entry-level luxury that will join the third upper-end family."[6] Does any real customer know what this means? Does anyone actually walk into a dealership and ask to see the midrange luxury vehicles?

Organizing by price point reinforces the madness of old-fashioned "good-better-best" marketing. This approach divides a brand's offerings into degrees of price-based "value." It says that a brand has 1) a low-end, cheap, poorer quality offering that is probably not a very good value yet affordable; 2) a mid-level, somewhat higher-priced, higher-level quality offering that is a slightly better value but slightly more expensive; and 3) the best offering in terms of quality and value but at a higher price.

No one really wants to think they bought a poor value product because it was the lowest price. Customers want to believe they purchased the best value for their needs. Some brands target their "value brands" for the so-called "value-conscious" consumer. Are these marketers thinking that consumers who pay a premium price are not value-conscious; they do not care about value? Every consumer is value-conscious, and this includes those who pay super premium prices. People value different things for different needs. What these price-point marketers fail to take into account is the fact that everyone wants to think they have purchased the best value for their particular need in their particular circumstances within the set of brands they can afford. (This is not to say that "good-better-best" has never been a successful approach, for Sears used it in its heyday. Now, however, the Sears story is a retail tragedy.[7]) To some people, a Prius is the best value for them. And for others, a Lexus is the best value for their needs. As Professor Robert H. Frank said in his Upshot column in the *New York Times*, "Clearly many rich people like to display their wealth. Yet, generally, they think they know value when they see it." He continued," The rich, of course, are willing to spend more, often a lot more, for products that deliver quality improvements they value. But few of them want to throw money away."[8]

When marketers focus market segmentation based solely on price, they demean the brand, creating brand commoditization through price management rather than brand management. Along with the automotive industry, the hotel industry still segments the market with terms such as *entry-level, mid-scale, upper-mid-scale, upscale,* and *luxury*. This allows people in the industry to communicate with each other, but, labels such as these make no sense to customers. Do customers actually score points with their significant other by saying, "I made a reservation for us at a mid-scale hotel for Valentine's Day"? Create strategies that are customer focused, not industry focused.

Unfortunately for brands, price segmentation educates the customer that mere availability and price are what matter. This leads to brand commoditization within a price category. It sets the stage for third-party online shopping channels that sort brands by price from lowest to highest within a set of specifications and without regard to brand differentiation. For example, sites like Expedia Hotels.com lead to the unintended consequence of self-commoditization driven by price-focused segmentation.

Price segmentation is not customer-centric. People want positive branded experiences of value. Overemphasis on deal only decreases a brand's stature by further emphasizing that the brand is cheap rather than a superior value. Customer-focused segmentation should be *needs* based, not price based. What are my needs? What problems do I have that need solutions? Which brand promises and delivers the best value for satisfying these needs? In an interview with the CEO of Haier, the Chinese appliance company and now world leader in business innovation, the interviewer pointed to the repositioning of Haier as a provider of solutions to consumers' problems selling not just home appliances, but also service such as water safety and other "quality of life" services.[9]

Quality

What about quality? It is a huge subject that refers more to delivering identified quality and service specifications. We define quality as the consistent delivery of the expected experience. When it comes to the customers' perceived brand value equation, quality refers to the entire brand experience. Price plays an important role in suggesting or implying inherent quality. Price perception affects quality perception. A 1996 article determined that lower price suggested lower quality, whereas higher price denoted higher quality.[10] There are also limits to how high or low a price can be.

> "Consumer intent on a purchase has two price limits in mind: an upper limit above which the article would be judged too expensive, and a lower limit below which the quality of the item would be suspect. This means that outside the limits price acts as the supreme indicator of quality. There is distrust for brands priced below the lower limit."[11]

Customers are affected by changing demographics, increasing globalization, localization, personalization, "The Age of I" mentality, the changing nature of family and relationships, and the decline in trust. Looking at prices relative to other prices is now easy because of the Internet with pervasive ratings, rankings, and sharing of experiences. Assessing brand worth is different than it was even a decade ago. As times have changed, so has the way in which customers assess brand value.

Here is a brief discussion of how customer-perceived brand value has morphed since the 1950s.[12]

The Evolution of Value

The underlying concept of value has not changed. It is the simple relationship of what you get for what you pay.

In the 1950s, marketers focused on features for the money as the synonym for value. The less money spent by the customer for particular features, the greater the value.

An example might be a lower cost for a quarter-inch drill. The 5¢ and 10¢ store was a special place with all sorts of items for 10 cents or less.

Pepsi-Cola had a slogan from 1939–1950: "Twice as much for a nickel."[13] The post-war 1950s were a time when mass marketing of foodstuffs to appliances was the norm. *Availability* and *affordability* and *new* were the guiding principles of consumption. This was the era when price alone was considered value.

This changed in the 1960s as marketers recognized the important role of functional benefits. As Professor Ted Levitt famously emphasized, customers do not buy a quarter-inch drill; they buy the benefit of quarter-inch holes. The danger of focusing on features rather than functions is that features can become outdated and replaced. (Technology companies face this situation all the time. Telecommunications companies created a dreadful commodity situation in which the focus is on availability of minutes/data for money.) Functional benefits endure.[14]

Snickers once emphasized the distinguishing feature in its recipe: "Comes up peanuts slice after slice." Mars evolved this promise to the enduring functional benefit of satisfying intrusive hunger. The revised slogan for years was, "Packed with peanuts, Snickers really satisfies." Over the years, the slogan has evolved, but the promise of hunger satisfaction has endured.

Over the years, book retailers like Barnes & Noble built their brands based on large assortments of books in their huge stores. These features delivered through a retail store are obsolete now. Amazon delivers greater inventory than any store could possibly deliver without a single store. The typewriter industry has disappeared, but the customer's need to communicate by creating documents remains. Creating documents via word-processing software satisfies the document creation need better.

In 1968, a landmark article in marketing launched the new concept of benefit segmentation.[15] Using toothpaste as an example, the author identified benefit segmentation such as flavor and taste, brightness of teeth, and decay prevention. Although features have certainly changed over the years and new benefits have arisen, such as prevention of gum disease, these original benefits still exist. So, during the 1970s, marketers increasingly defined value as distinctive functional benefits for the money.

In the 1980s, the pace of life quickened. People lived life in the fast lane. Time, modern life's scarcest resource, entered the picture as a component of value. Time is a precious resource, spoken of in the same terms as we speak of money: I save time, I spend time, I use my time wisely, I budget my time, I love time-savers, and so forth. We were experiencing the throes of "time famine." How much leisure time do I really have? Am I working more than usual?" People began to feel that they did not have enough time. (Remember the lyrics, "Time keeps on slippin', slippin', slippin', into the future")?[16] The reaction was to seek brands that offered the gift of time. So consumers viewed value as functional benefits divided by both money and time.

With two-income families, avoidance of physical or psychological effort became part of the customer's perceived value of a branded product or service. The energy needed to choose and use a brand became an important consideration. Effort is a cost just like money and time. How difficult is it going to be to make a choice? How convenient is it to buy? How easy is it to use the product and service? Make it simple. Make it easy. Make it effortless.

As markets have evolved, customers have come to view a brand experience as more than just functional benefits. They want products and services that are good, and they want to feel good, too. Emotions are valued as part of the total branded experience. Emotional benefits are a multidimensional concept. "I don't just want to buy a Happy Meal at McDonald's because my kid likes the toy. I also want to feel I am being a good mother concerned with what my children eat and drink."

Social Benefits

With the enormous increase in social connectivity enabled by the Internet, there is now the increased importance of social benefits. Social benefits include the familiar benefits such as status, reputation, and belonging. Social benefits recognize our social communities, our kindred spirits, and our propensity for amassing "friends" and "likes." The total brand experience consists of a combination of functional, emotional, and social benefits.

As we examined in the Age of I discussion, social benefits satisfy our needs for belonging to groups sharing our interests or values. Social benefits also take into account social perceptions such as status and self-image. Importantly, social benefits reflect our increasing desire for social responsibility on the part of brands and companies as well as of ourselves.

Perceived brand value is a complex, multidimensional combination of the total experience I get (functional, emotional, and social benefits) relative to what I pay (money, time, and effort).

Along with all these evolutions, customers today have added one more critical element: trust. Maybe it is because we tend to deal anonymously with so many digital and virtual entities that we need to feel that we have trust before making a purchase or commitment. Maybe it is the decline in institutional trust that has forced us to look elsewhere for it. Maybe it is the trust we place in our friends' opinions versus the trust (or lack of) we have in companies and brand claims. In a world of declining trust, brands must be trustworthy to deliver value. We have become trust seekers in a world where institutional trust is shrinking.

Trust as a Multiplier

Today's value equation includes trust as a multiplier. Being trustworthy means delivering on promises. Being trustworthy means that a company and brand behaves with integrity. Trustworthy means that a customer believes in the predictability of the branded experience.

We call this new value equation Trustworthy Brand Value (see Figure 4.2). It is the total brand experience of functional, emotional, and social benefits relative to the costs of money, time, and effort with trust as an overall multiplier. If trust in the brand is high, the perceived brand value is increased. If trust in the brand is low, the perceived brand value is low. If there is no trust, it does not matter what the benefits or the costs are; if trust is zero, the value is zero.

Steve Hall, CEO of driversselect.com, a used car dealership in Dallas, says that being transparent about financial terms builds trust. He finds that most dealerships are reluctant to provide the openness necessary to gain trust that is needed for a purchase. The lowest price is not everything.[17]

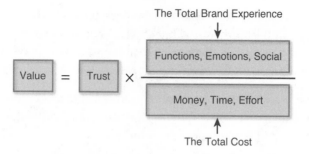

Figure 4.2 Trustworthy Brand Value

One-Think Shopping

Trustworthy Brand Value addresses one of the more interesting paradoxes of today's shopping experience: the desire for multiple choices and the desire for ease of choice. People desire choice, yet having too much choice increases uncertainty, decreases speed of decision-making, and requires more physical and mental effort. Consumers want more choices, but they want choosing to be easier. One-Think Shopping[18] alleviates the uncertainty of too much choice while helping a consumer choose wisely. With One-Think Shopping, the consumer can quickly make decisions based on the trustworthiness of the brand. It is a streamlined roadway through the cluttered confusion of choices. This trustworthiness is part of the brand's value.

By building Trustworthy Brand Value, a marketer enables one-think decision-making because the customer does not have to think twice about the brand choice. If the customer trusts that the expected total branded experience will be delivered for the costs of money, time, and effort, the purchase decision will be easier to make. One of the key benefits of this new approach to value is "One-Think Shopping." It means that, all things being equal, all brand ties should end in your favor.

Need for Simplicity

There is the desire for simplicity in this sea of excessive choice. People want more choices, but they also want simplicity in making choices. The brand and corporate identity company Siegel & Gale issues a Global

Brand Simplicity Index each year. Its main point: Make life simple. Marketers must simplify the ways in which they communicate with customers. Simplicity pays. Where many companies act on the perception that the world is too complex for simplicity, Siegel & Gale believe that the opposite is true.[19]

Trustworthy Brand Value recognizes that the dichotomy of simplicity and complexity of choice is not an either/or situation. People want to maximize both: they want available multiple choices because they enhance individuality. At the same time, they want the decision-making process to be simple and easy. No one wants to make a poor decision, and no one wants to waste time making decisions. Building Trustworthy Brand Value means maximizing the intersection of this paradox.

Steve Jobs understood that complex things could be simplified through design. His product was complicated, but the experience he provided wasn't. He used to say, "Simplicity is the ultimate sophistication."[20] And, in fact, this is how Trustworthy Brand Value helps your brand create One-Think Shopping: by driving all the elements of the new value equation, the complexity of choice becomes easier.

In an interesting discussion of the new ways of shopping, with growing numbers of shoppers no longer browsing in-store (the end of impulse shopping, say the writers), the authors talk about the importance of painlessness in the shopping experience (a new rule of shopping). The Web is helping us avoiding the "pain" of shopping, such as the dejection of arriving and not seeing your choice on the showroom floor or shelf. One-Think Shopping is a pain avoidance mechanism. The brand helps me choose so I do not have to give this purchase a second thought. I am over with this shopping.[21]

Deal Loyalty versus Real Loyalty

Building brand value is about more than communicating 1) a brand promise, 2) your brand's costs, and 3) the drivers of your brand's trust. It is also about 4) how a brand communicates its value. A brand cannot build value though mere deal manipulation. This harms the brand and sullies the brand-customer relationship by avoiding satisfaction of needs.

Pursuing price and driving deals do not create real loyalists. Overemphasis on deals attracts customers who are deal loyal, not brand loyal. Generating sales based solely on deals is brand detrimental. It is a hole from which it is hard to extricate a brand. Excessive emphasis on price and incentives has significant negative impact on a brand. The "let's make a deal" approach is death-knell, deleterious marketing. Deal loyalty demolishes brand value. Constantly offering deals extracts value from the brand, weakening it over time. The more deals, the more price sensitive the customer; the more price sensitive the customer, the deeper the deal discount needs to be.

Of course, a "deal" can generate traffic, such as coupons on Groupon or Living Social. Deals are especially appropriate to attract new customers and to encourage repeat purchases. But living with dealing creates customers who will leave the brand the minute another brand has a better deal. Marketers need to differentiate between bargain hunters who are deal loyalists, not real loyalists.

Relationships are built on trust. Partnership theory rests on the idea that trust is at the core of strong relationships. In today's world where so many transactions and conversations are with unseen people or groups, trust has become the primary condition for belief in brand connections, which eventually translate into truly committed customers. Unlike deal-driven, price-focused, brand-indifferent, short-term attachments, committed brand relationships are enduring profitable brand relationships.

The Collaborative Three-Box Model drives the building of enduring, profitable brand relationships. It is customer-centric, focusing on generating real loyalty across geography. As with the ideas that are altering our world and the forces that are requiring us to change our marketing ways, the imperative of growing Trustworthy Brand Value is transformative. Global brands need an approach that takes all these into account. The Collaborative Three-Box Model is that new approach.

Endnotes

1. Adams, Will, Johnson, and Jack Hody, Black Eyed Peas, "Gone Going," *Monkey Business*, BMG Sapphire Songs, Bubble Toes Publishing, I Am Composing LLC, 2005.

2. Tybout, Alice and Sternthal, Brian, "Mastering Marketing, Part 2: Integrating Positioning Perspectives," *Financial Times*, September 28, 1998.

3. Strom, Stephanie, "McDonald's Tests Custom Burgers and Other New Concepts as Sales Drop," *New York Times*, January 24, 2015.

4. For a discussion of the Fair Value Corridor see Light, Larry and Kiddon, Joan, *Six Rules for Brand Revitalization: Learn How Companies Like McDonald's Can Re-Energize Their Brands*, Pearson Education, Inc. Wharton School Publishing, NJ, 2009, p. 118.

5. Day, George, *Market Driven Strategy, Processes for Creating Value*, 1990.

6. Kurylko, Diana, "Jag-Land Rover's 2017 Sales Goal? Half of M-B," *Automotive News*, November 3, 2014.

7. See various articles such as Solomon, Steven Davidoff, "As Sears Gasps, Lambert Turns to Financial Engineering," *New York Times*, November 12, 2014, and Heard on the Street column, "Sears Still Can't Call Itself a Store of Value," *Wall Street Journal*, November 8–9, 2014.

8. Frank, Robert H., "Conspicuous Consumption? Yes, But It's Not Crazy," The Upshot, *New York Times*, November 23, 2014.

9. Kleiner, Art, "The Thought Leader Interview: Zhang Ruimin," *Strategy & Business*, Issue 77, Winter 2014, pp. 96–102.

10. Gabor, Andre, and Graner, C. W. J., "Price as an Indicator of Quality," *The London School of Economics and Political Science: Economica*, New Series, Vol. XXXIII, No. 129, February 1966.

11. Gabor, Andre, and Graner, C. W. J., "Price as an Indicator of Quality," *The London School of Economics and Political Science: Economica*, New Series, Vol. XXXIII, No. 129, February 1966.

12. An early discussion about the evolving nature of "value" can be found in "The New Value Equation," *Stores Magazine*, January 1995.

13. See Wikipedia, Pepsi-Cola.

14. Levitt, Theodore, "Marketing Myopia," *Harvard Business Review*, July/August 1960, vol. 38, pp. 57–66.

15. Haley, Russ, "Benefit Segmentation—A Decision-Oriented Research Tool," *Journal of Marketing*, July 1968, Vol. 32, pp. 30-36.

16. Miller, Steve, The Steve Miller Band, "Fly Like an Eagle," *Fly Like an Eagle*, 1977.

17. Sawyers, Arlena, "Financial Openness Can Beat the Lowest Pricing, Dealer Says," *Automotive News*, November 17, 2014.

18. Since the 1990s, when we were involved with the Coalition for Brand Equity (CBE), we have presented this idea of brand as a signal for easier choice selection.

19. Elliott, Stuart, "Seeing a Value in Simplicity," *New York Times*, October 29, 2014.

20. Pollack, John, "See the Analogies, Change the World," *Wall Street Journal*, November 8–9, 2014.

21. Banjo, Shelly and Germano, Sara, "The End of the Impulse Shopper," *Wall Street Journal*, November 25, 2014.

5

Build Brand Trust

Trust yourself
Trust yourself to know the way that will prove true in the end
Trust yourself
Trust yourself to find the path where there is no if and when
Don't trust me to show you the truth
When the truth may only be ashes and dust
If you want somebody you can trust, trust yourself

—Bob Dylan[1]

Trust in a World of Distrust and Mistrust

Bob Dylan has a knack for seeing the future. Today, consumers prefer to trust themselves, check with peers, or go to rating and ranking sites for information they can trust. It used to be that you could "trust your car to the man who wears the star,"[2] as Texaco used to describe its brand. Or, "You can be sure if it's Westinghouse."[3] Or, "If it's Borden's it's got to be good."[4] Or, "The Watch The World Has Learned To Trust...Omega."[5]

Slogans claiming, "trust me," do not work in an increasingly informed, questioning, skeptical, and demanding society. Trust cannot be claimed; it must be earned. People turn to their friends and their peers for opinions and recommendations. And, in many instances, people trust the opinions of people they do not even know for ratings and reviews.

According to an April 2012 study from Nielsen, the global research company, "92 percent of consumers around the world say they trust "earned" media, such as word-of-mouth or recommendations from friends and family, above all other forms of advertising—an increase of

18 percent since 2007." Online consumer reviews are the second most trusted source of brand information and messaging, with 70 percent of global consumers surveyed online indicating they trust messages on this platform, an increase of 15 percent in four years."[6]

Millennials are especially prone to relying on their social networks' user-generated content as a trustworthy resource instead of experts, brands, governments, or other traditional establishments.[7] This newfound trust in social networks and online sources does not just affect Millennials, however. The 2014 Edelman Trust Barometer pointed out that:

> "When it comes to first sources of information, respondents rated online, newspapers and television relatively evenly for both general business information and breaking news about business.

> "Perhaps more revealing than level of trust in sources for first finding information is level of trust in sources for confirming or validating information about business. On this question, respondents rated online search 16 points higher (36%) than television and 17 points higher than newspapers."[8]

People around the world have lost trust in institutions. The report from *Global Monitor* in 2013 stated that currently we are experiencing "high levels of distrust in public authorities, ...declining trust in business, ...hand-in-hand with an increasing prominence in social networks ...."[9] Additionally, *Global Monitor* points out that its global data shows a sad story when it comes to big business maximizing "profits at the expense of community and consumers," and "politicians today are incompetent or corrupt."[10]

In 2012, Gartner, the technology research group, published a "white paper" on the top trends for the future. Number 7 was "Renegotiation of Consumer Trust." Gartner pointed out then what now seems to be more of a commonplace way of living than a coming trend.

> "The consumer market is seeking new institutions, brands and values to trust in. The collapse of confidence in traditional institutions following bank failures, government collapse, corruption, economic and civil unrest and the disruption

to previously accepted "norms" (such as local communities and nuclear families) have sent consumers searching for new brands, values and social organizations that they can trust. Brands that help their customers through hard times can build strong emotional and cognitive loyalty among consumers, leading to significant opportunity for brand extension."[11]

Brand management that leverages the three forces of increased globalization, localization, and personalization can help to increase trust. The familiarity and ubiquity of global brands can build trust. People are more comfortable with brands that are familiar. It is comforting to recognize a familiar brand when visiting Japan, Germany, or Australia. It is a common expression that "familiarity breeds contempt." In fact, "familiarity breeds comfort." Brands that are preferred worldwide can have a trust perception advantage. BA built its brand revitalization around the claim that it was "the world's favourite airline." However, globalization is also perceived as a threat to many consumers. So brand managers must be vigilant that standardization does not make a brand less relevant and differentiated.

It is interesting to check the results of *The Reader's Digest Asia Trusted Brands* survey. In 2013, the *Business Times* (Singapore) reported that in Singapore many local brands were more trusted than global brands. Thirty-seven percent (or 41 out of 110) of trusted brands were local brands. As the commercial director for *Reader's Digest* stated,

> "The increasing number of local SMEs gaining brand recognition and trust is a significant achievement.... Successful local brands help enhance our economic growth, boost exports and raise awareness of the Singapore brand in other markets."[12]

Definitions of Trust

The literature on trust is vast and sometimes complex. Social scientists, market researchers, political analysts, psychiatrists and psychologists, academics, and others view trust as an essential element for any type of relationship building. Because of all this scrutiny and investigation, trust has many definitions.

Garbino and Johnson, in a review of the roles of satisfaction and trust, point out the wide agreement that trust is "an essential ingredient for successful relationships." They acknowledge that there are many different definitions of trust. Some define trust as "a willingness to rely on an exchange partner in whom one has confidence." Others define trust as the perception of "confidence in the exchange partner's reliability and integrity." Garbino and Johnson propose that an expectation of trustworthiness results from the ability to perform (expertise), reliability, and intentionality. All definitions "highlight the importance of confidence and reliability in the conception of trust."[13]

Based on the numerous definitions and volumes of academic work on trust, there is broad agreement that trust plays an increasingly central role in building a strong, durable, profitable, growing brand. We define trust as the confidence you have relying on the brand to live up to its promises and its reputation of authority based on leadership, credibility, integrity, and responsibility.

Two Kinds of Trust

It is valuable to distinguish between brand trust and organizational trust. Brand trust is the trust that people have in the specific product or service brand. Organizational trust is the trust that people have in the organization that produces the brand. Building both must be a focus of any organization.

Some organizations share the corporate name with a product or service brand such as Ford Motor Company and Ford Division; Marriott and Marriott Hotel brand; Electrolux AB and Electrolux appliances; Coca-Cola company and the Coca-Cola brand; General Electric and GE jet engines; Nike and Nike shoes; Campbell's and Campbell's soup. When product/service brands share the same name with the corporate parent, the product/service brand should focus on the relevant differentiated promise of the particular offer while the "parent" brand stands for authority based on the leadership, credibility, integrity, and responsibility of the organization.

Over the decades, we have stated that a brand is a promise of a relevant and differentiated experience. A brand is a promise of future intent:

I will deliver this to you.[14] Trust is about the future, too. It brings the authority of credibility, integrity, leadership, and responsibility to the promised brand experience. So brand trust is an important decision-making driver; it is the multiplier in the new customer-perceived value equation: Trustworthy Brand Value.

Brand Trust

Let's focus on brand trust first. Some define brand trust "as an important mediating factor on the customer behaviors before and after the purchase of the product; and they say it causes long-term loyalty strengthening the relation between two parties. Brand trust can be defined as the willingness of the consumer to rely on the ability of the brand to perform its stated functions."[15]

How is a brand different from a product or service? A brand is a promise of a relevant, differentiated branded experience. The actual product or service experience is evidence of the truth of that promise. Failure to deliver the expectation forces the customer to question the trustworthiness of the brand. When a Swiffer Duster says that it is a dust magnet, people expect the dust to be off the shelf after use. And, as Swiffer depicts in advertising, if a little old lady or a one-armed young man finds it easy and safe to use, even better. If the One World flight alliance says its network of airlines provides a single, seamless "world" for flying internationally, customers expect BA to honor the American Airlines ticket, seating, class of service, and so on, and vice versa. Make promises you can deliver, and deliver the promises you make. Customers are not expecting a challenging world of surprises and disappointments.

Service brands have the added dimension of relying on people to deliver all or part of the service experience and to personalize all or part of the service experience. Companies manufacture product brands in a factory and sell these in a package in a retail environment (brick and mortar or online): quality control is built into the manufacturing and packaging systems. Computers and floor managers can monitor zero defects. Algorithms, stocking plan-o-grams, and logistics manage the sales. Service brands depend on a person. One hopes that the sales clerk at H&M or the bank teller at Royal Bank of Canada has had a good morning before showing up for work. When United Airlines says its skies are friendly, travelers expect "friendliness" from gate agents to flight attendants regardless of whether these employees have had their coffee. If the promise is not delivered, customers lose trust.

Believing that a product or a service and brand are interchangeable ideas is a mistake. A brand is about an experience that a customer will have. If you think of your brand as a product or service rather than an experience, you are limited when it comes to refreshing that brand to keep it relevant. This is why having a visionary Brand Ambition is so important. Amazon began as an online bookstore and reinforced that in communications: the world's largest bookstore." But Jeff Bezos was prescient and saw that this was limiting not just for the Amazon brand but for any brand extensions such as Amazon Cloud.

In our previous book, we used Crest as an example. Crest went from cavity prevention for its toothpaste to a lifetime of superior oral care. This allowed for brand extensions.[16] P&G has accomplished the same thing with Tide. Tide used to just be powdered detergent for clean clothes. (Tide was so powerful at cleaning clothes that a dirty sock in a sock in a little boy's pants pocket—"a sock in a sock in a pocket"—became really clean.) If you want more than just clean clothes, Bold 2 in 1 combined the effectiveness of laundry detergent and fabric softener. If you want your clothes to have an out-of-the ordinary scent, Gain promised a "whole new scent universe." Today, Tide promises to clean and care for clothes through an extended line of products. Aside from powders, liquids, and pods, there are various versions of clean that you can have from Tide, including Tide for sports clothing, Tide for superior stain release, Tide for cleaning in cold water, Tide with bleach for whitest clothes, and ingredient branding such as Tide with Febreeze, Tide with Downy, and Tide with Oxy from Oxyclean. Febreeze is available in Gain laundry scents, and Swiffer Wet Jet Pads are available in Febreeze scents. The key to effective line extensions is that they are all consistent with the relevant, differentiated promise of the overall brand. The principle is straightforward: deliver what you promise and promise what you deliver; otherwise, trust erodes.

To know what to deliver, it is critical to make sure the cross-functional team (CFT) has clearly defined the Brand Ambition. Then the CFT must ensure that all Collaborative Three-Box Model activities in Boxes 1, 2, and 3 reflect this Brand Ambition. The Brand Plan to Win, both global and regional, begins with Brand Purpose for a reason. What you want the brand to be matters. It guides all thought, strategies, actions, and behavior. Strategies and actions consistent with the Brand Ambition help to build trust.

Organizational Trust

A corporate brand plays a different role than the product or service brand. How customers perceive the corporate brand has an effect on the product and service brands. Why? The corporate brand represents the overarching identification of organizational trust. There are some who define the value of a corporate brand as "the promise of an organization (i.e., the covenant aspect of the corporation) which provides sameness and credibility about its organization to all its stakeholders."[17]

Organizational trust (trust in the corporate brand) is also an important decision-making driver, but the stakeholders are different. Do employees and potential employees trust the company to live up to its promises? Does the financial community trust the organization to live up to expectations? Do owner-operators or franchisees trust that a relationship with the organization will be as promised? Does society trust that the organization will behave sustainably and responsibly?

Corporate brand trust is a commitment not just to customers, but to all stakeholders: shareholders, financial communities, employees, owners, owner-operators, franchisees, strategic partners, suppliers, and other constituencies on global, national, and local bases. Corporate brand trust is a vital, strategic element of corporate reputation. The more customers trust the corporation, the more open they are to buying products and services from that corporation's brands. The more investors and the financial community trust the corporation, the more willing they are to invest in it and support its strategies and projects. This puts trust into a brand's trust bank. If customers do not trust the brand owner, trust in the brand will be lower, and there will be diminished ability to bounce back from a crisis.

"During the 1970s, Al Golin, Chairman of Golin Harris, and Ray Kroc, founder of McDonald's, developed the concept of the trust bank, meaning companies should make deposits of goodwill to draw upon in times of crisis."[18] When a brand or an organization builds trust, that trust is accrued and deposited—just like money—into a trust bank. When there is a crisis, this accrued trust can tide you through the bad times, especially if the customers or stakeholders are committed to the brand or organization. With institutional trust declining, it is more and more important that trust be seen as part of a brand's worth.

Trust and the Value Equation

For product and service brands, as we discussed, the first step is to understand the drivers of trust for managing the new value equation: Trustworthy Brand Value. Remember, in the customer's new mind-set, a brand's value is a function of what he receives (functional, emotional, social benefits) for what it costs him (money, time, effort), with trust as the value equation multiplier. If there is no trust, there is no value, because any amount times zero is zero. If there is a lot of trust, the perceived value of the brand is increased.

The current debates in the EU regarding Google and the potential for anti-trust legislation has some pundits worrying that Google will fight the legislations. Microsoft fought for years, and its reputation took a hit. Google can fight, too. But will winning the anti-trust battle hurt the brand's trusted reputation?[19]

Trust Capital

Building corporate trust is an increasingly relevant activity for organizations globally. For example, it is clearly on the Tesco agenda as the new CEO focuses on returning the brand to a credible, admired, respected entity among customers and stakeholders. Along with closing nonperforming stores and reviewing the pension scheme, rebuilding trust is a stated goal to help Tesco return to its British retailing glory. Trust generates value, and value drives organizational wealth.

Capital comes in three forms: Financial Capital, Intellectual Capital, and Human Capital. There is an important fourth component of organizational wealth: Trust Capital. We define Trust Capital as the customer confidence in the authority, credibility, integrity, leadership, and responsibility of an organization to deliver promises of value to stakeholders.[20] Trust Capital creates value for the organization. It is what an organization can draw from during troubling times or crises. In a world of diminishing institutional trust, Trust Capital is by far the most important piece of organizational wealth for twenty-first century organizations.

The *Edelman Trust Barometer* supports this. In 2014, the *Barometer* indicated that focusing on operational excellence, along with products and services, was not as important as focusing on engagement and integrity issues. The attributes of operational excellence have now become "table-stakes" while the attributes of how customers and employees are treated are more important. "The 2014 results reinforce this proposition that business has left trust opportunities on the table over the past year." Edelman concluded that, based on the data, business should be focused on the underperforming areas with the highest priorities such as ethics, openness, transparency, and putting customers ahead of profits.[21] Just as trust brings economic security, psychological safety, and social stability to governments, Trust Capital brings organizational confidence, steadiness, and hopefulness in the future potential of the corporation.

Corporate Social Responsibility

An increasingly important way to build Trust Capital is through a focus on corporate social responsibility (CSR). Consumers today are concerned with more than just features, convenience, and price. They care about how they feel about the brand and about how they feel about the organization. "They also care about the social and environmental impacts of products. Indeed, many ask questions like: Does this toy contain toxic substances? Where do the materials in this garment come from? And are the production processes environmentally friendly?"[22]

More and more, corporations are being held to higher standards when it comes to their behavior toward people, places, and things. People expect that corporations need to produce results. But they also believe that businesses can do well and do good at the same time. This belief in "planet and people friendly good works" is particularly important among younger generations. Having a positive corporate brand reputation is a positive business advantage.

Furthermore, where once the C-suite discussions were about profitability versus responsibility and sustainability, today that discussion is a moot point. There was a time when CSR was questioned as to its ability to make money in the year for the year. Those times have changed. In an instant information, digital, mobile, 24/7 world, what you do relative to what you say is common knowledge. CEOs and their teams now recognize that it is in the company's best interest to maximize both profitability *and* responsibility at the same time.

Vaude, the family-owned mountain sports clothing maker in Germany, is one of these companies. It and its 1,600 employees "aspire to be the most sustainable outdoor brand in Europe." As the CEO, Antje von Dewitz, is quoted as saying, "Enterprises must take responsibility for actions towards their employees, the community or the environment." Living up to this promise, the company is about to release its first common good balance sheet—"a scorecard that awards participating companies points based on the extent to which they have acted in a human, co-operative, sustainable, just and democratic manner. There are minus points for violating labour standards, pollution, unequal pay for women and using tax havens." Developed by Christian Feber, the common good balance sheet has a list of 1,700 enrolled companies primarily in Germany, Austria, and Switzerland.[23] As Andrew Winston says in his book, "Sustainability can no longer be treated as a side department or a niche conversation within a business."[24]

While the concept of a strong corporate brand may have once been regarded as a nice thing to do, in today's environment, it is a crucial part of any large company's long-term strategy. Corporate brand trust is a foundational requirement that all organizations need to function more effectively. "Good growth" based on ethical behavior and sustainability must be a top priority for all CEOs.

According to Patrick Cescau, former CEO of Unilever and current chairman of the IHG board of directors, the "agenda of sustainability and corporate responsibility is not only central to business strategy but will increasingly become a critical driver of business growth.... I believe that how well and how quickly businesses respond to this agenda will determine which companies succeed and which will fail in the next few decades."[25]

Right Results the Right Way

With withering trust in institutions, it is vital to produce the right results by doing the right things in the right way. Having the right people is only the beginning. The right people must be aligned behind doing the right things in the right way producing the right results.

Doing the right things in the right way to produce the right results addresses these issues:

- What is the best way to build a corporate brand across geographies, brands, people, shareholders, franchisees, partners, suppliers, and local communities?

- What is the best way to ensure that corporate responsibility is integrated into all of an organization's decision-making?

- Is the organization a good global and local corporate citizen?

- How sustainable are its actions?

Make sure that the organizational sustainability opportunity is on the agenda. This means meeting the needs of customers, communities, and businesses without compromising the needs of future generations. Currently, both Google and IKEA are investing in renewable power such as wind farming. This "green energy" push is an action that is visible and credible, not just boardroom banter. "Technology companies' power hungry data centres have made them a target of environmental campaigners who are pushing the industry to move away from the fossil fuels driving climate changes."[26]

Being trustworthy is not what you claim. It is about being worthy of a customer's trust based on how you behave. It is not a mere cliché to say, "Actions speak louder than words." In today's reality it is a significant truth. What you see is much more important that what you say especially in the area of social responsibility. In the expanding realm of everyday reviews and the ubiquitous mobile phone camera, there is no place to hide. What an organization says and does is instantaneously available for all to see anywhere and at any time. Organizations and brands are instantly evaluated by what they are actually doing to make the world a better place. People's antennae identify those companies and brands that are saying the right things but not delivering them. And these companies can be pilloried in the Internet's town square in front of millions for hypocritical behaviors.

A Strong Corporate Brand

A strong corporate brand is built on a strong foundation of credibility, integrity, leadership, and responsibility. Corporate responsibility is an important pillar. It must be corporate-wide. Promoting responsibility as a true part of the business—and not a separate part of the business— makes the organization appear action oriented, putting sustainable deeds up front rather than as occasional afterthoughts.

Corporate responsibility is about demonstrating good corporate citizenship. It must be corporate-wide and not promoted as a separate part of the business. It must be in the veins of the organization as a whole.

Endnotes

1. Dylan, Bob, "Trust Yourself," *Empire Burlesque*, Special Ride Music, 1985.

2. In the 1960s, "You can trust your car to the man who wears the star" was the Texaco jingle. Check Wikipedia for the history of Texaco.

3. Began use of slogan 1954; see Wikipedia for Westinghouse Electric.

4. Slogan with Elsie mascot in use in 1945; Books.google.co/books: the Borden Company.

5. In use 1956; see Books.google.co/books: Omega.

6. "Global Survey of Trust in Advertising," www.nielsen.com/.../ global-trust-in-advertising, Nielsen, April 2012.

7. Refer to Chapter 2, "Globalization, Localization, Personalization," for the discussion on Millennials and trust.

8. Edelman Trust Barometer, Edelman Berland, 2014.

9. The Futures Company, "Global Energies," 2013.

10. The Futures Company, *2013 Global Monitor*.

11. Gartner, "10 Consumer Macro Trends to Impact Technology, Media and Service Providers for Next 10 Years," April 16, 2012.

12. "Local Brands More Trusted This Year; 37% of Brands Award Winners in Asia Are from Singapore," *The Business Times Singapore*, May 23, 2013.

13. Garbino, Ellen, and Johnson, Mark S., "The Different Roles of Satisfaction, Trust, and Commitment in Customer Relationships," *Journal of Marketing*, Vol. 63, No. 2, Spring 1999.

14. See examples in speeches such as Light, Larry, "Brand Journalism," *Advertising Age*, June 2004; Light Larry, "Brand Journalism," *ANA*, October 2004; article, Light, Larry, "Trust Is a Must," *ANA Advertiser*, Winter 2004.

15. Geçti, Faith and Zengin, Hayrettin, "The Relationship between Brand Trust, Brand Affect, Attitudinal Loyalty and Behavioral Loyalty: A Field Study towards Sports Shoe Consumers in Turkey," *International Journal of Marketing Studies*, Vol. 15, No. 2, April 2013.

16. Light, Larry and Kiddon, Joan, *Six Rules for Brand Revitalization: Learn How Companies Such as McDonald's Can Re-Energize Their Brands*, Wharton School Publishing, Pearson Education, Inc., NJ, 2009, p. 33.

17. Hamzah, Zalfa Laili and Sharifah Faridah Syed Alwi Brunel, "Designing Corporate Brand Experience in an Online Context," *Journal of Business Research*, Vol. 67, No. 11, November 2014.

18. Heath, Robert, ed., *The Encyclopedia of Public Relations, SAGE Publications*, 2005.

19. Lex, "Google: Trust and Antitrust," *Financial Times*, November 26, 2014.

20. For the role of trust in rebuilding brands, see Light, Larry and Kiddon, Joan, *Six Rules for Brand Revitalization: Learn How Companies Such as McDonald's Can Re-Energize Their Brands*, Wharton School Publishing, Pearson Education, Inc., NJ, 2009, Chapter 7. Also see Light, Larry, "Trust Is a Must," *ANA Advertiser*, Winter 2004.

21. *Edelman Trust Barometer*, Edelman Berland, 2014.

22. Odenwald, Thomas and Berg, Christian, "A New Perspective on Enterprise Resource Management," *MIT Sloan Management Review*, Fall 2014, Vol. 56. No. 1.

23. Bryant, Chris, "A Corporate Balance Sheet with a Little Added Love," *Financial Times*, November 20, 2014.

24. Elkington, John, "Sustainability," *Strategy & Business*, Issue 77, Winter 2014, p. 89.

25. Cescau, Patrick, Group Chief Executive of Unilever, speech at the 2007 INDEVOR Alumni Forum in INSEAD, Fontainebleau, France May 25, 2007.

26. Clark, Pilita, "Google and IKEA Step Up the Green Energy Drives with Wind Farm Deals," *Financial Times*, November 19, 2014.

PART II

The Collaborative
Three-Box Model

6

The Evolution of Global Marketing and The New Collaborative Three-Box Model

If you don't know where you're going, any road will take you there.

—George Harrison[1]

In the previous chapters, we discussed the challenges that marketers and brands face in our changing world. We examined the forces affecting how marketing must readapt itself. We also looked at the customer's new perception of brand value—Trustworthy Brand Value—and the need to build brand trust and corporate trust. The thinking in these previous chapters creates the driving context for The Collaborative Three-Box Model. Now we explain why it is essential that current approaches to managing brands must change to build and grow successful brands.

Organizational Implications

What road do we need to take? What do organizations and brand leaders need to do differently? What are the key disciplines that must be put into place? What are the mind-set and job definition changes that must occur? In an increasingly global, local, and personal world, these organizational choices for managing brands are a current senior executive topic. Some of the internal, enterprise debates revolve around issues such as globalization versus localization versus personalization, standardization versus fractionalization, centralization versus decentralization. These topics alone require great deliberation, consideration, and discussion leading to organizational changes of great magnitude. If a company's self-perception is that of a sales company, it will be organized as a sales company and power will be with those in sales. If a company sees itself as an engineering company, it is organized around the engineers. If a company is brand focused but centralized, then power is in the center. Brands thrive when the organization is designed to enhance them. Brands need an organizational model that focuses personnel on building them for enduring profitable growth. The Collaborative Three-Box Model is just such an enterprise design.

To fully grasp why we believe The Collaborative Three-Box Model is so necessary for today's brands, let's look back at the evolution of global marketing and the road that leads us to where we are now. Understanding the past helps us see the future better.[2] (Refer to Figure 1.3 in Chapter 1, "Overview: A New Approach to Global Marketing.")

The One-Box Model: Global Standardization

Thirty years ago, in 1983, Professor Theodore Levitt, a professor at Harvard Business School, published another landmark article in the May/June issue of *Harvard Business Review*. The article was titled "The Globalization of Marketing."[3] Professor Levitt asserted that well-managed companies must offer globally standardized products that are advanced, functional, reliable, and low priced. Multinational companies should not concentrate on idiosyncratic consumer preferences but instead focus on global commonalities. His premise was that a global brand should be the same everywhere regardless of culture, language, customs, and values. His idea of globalization fortified the thinking that global brands must do the following:

- Have one standardized, global positioning
- Have a single globally standardized product or service
- Ensure that the product or service is supported by a single expression and execution of this brand positioning; everything is uniform and unvarying

The result of this rationale was that a global, central marketing function—usually in the headquarters and with the lead agencies reporting to the headquarters—created the brand proposition, strategic direction, product design, executional guidelines, and policies as well as all internal and external marketing communications. The center did it all. The role of the local markets was to merely execute the global directions.

The primary argument for this globally standardized method was the increased cost efficiency of having a single, centralized standardized approach. The center was the seat of all brand authority. It became the global police force ensuring compliance around the world.

In addition to cost savings, another common argument for centralization is quality control, with the emphasis on control. There is no question that certain "standards" need to be adopted across geography, especially when it comes to things such as safety or sustainability of resources or treatment of workers. When it comes to marketing, centralization promises to set a minimum standard of quality but does not take into account relevant local differences. And it creates a sense of overarching good management because the center did not believe that the regions could manage the agreed quality standards.

The real premise for excessive centralized control is often a lack of trust. People in the center do not trust that the local markets will do the right thing. With no trust, the center takes control of local implementation and takes local resources away from the local markets. It is not uncommon to hear executives in the center say that central control is essential because those in the field or the regions are not as capable as those in headquarters.

The outcome of this "superiority" attitude created globally centralized yet insensitive brand dictatorships. The mind-set was, "Don't stray from the template. Don't play with the template." The Collaborative Three-Box Model cannot operate well without trust. True, the trust must be earned. But in The Model, everyone is working together and learning what the opposing positions are in advance of decision-making. The debates and teamwork earn trust because these challenges change the mind-set of distrust.

Global standardization is what we refer to as a "One-Box Model." There was one brand management box: the globally bred and led brand management box. The whole world was confined to and force-fitted into one common brand box. When introduced, it was a forceful look at the globe and how to communicate well around it. This branded blanket globalization had some successes; we already mentioned British

Airways' "World's Favourite Airline" as one of these. Some cosmetic brands, such as Estée Lauder, use this approach effectively, but these are the exceptions.

In an adaptation of his article for the *McKinsey Quarterly*, Theodore Levitt said, "Different cultural preferences, national tastes...are vestiges of the past."[4] As we described earlier, with the alterations shaping our changing world, it is clear that such a position of standardized homogenized marketing for today and tomorrow is definitely, and worryingly, wrong. With all the fragmentation, segmentation, and fractionalization already happening, homogenization is hazardous for brand health. The significance of localization and personalization demands that brands be structured and managed in ways that reflect a cultural, social, and economic sense of place as well as personal preferences and differences.

Brands in the 1980s did not need to live in a 24/7, digital, mobile, networked existence to notice that the One-Box Model was stifling accessibility and creativity. Although globally standardized marketing is efficient, it became clear that for too many brands, it was not optimally effective. Efficient use of limited resources is always a necessity and should always be a consideration. But for many brands, there was a recognition that this One-Box Model approach was leading to lowest common denominator thinking: thinking that was acceptable everywhere and particularly relevant nowhere. The inevitable result of the arrogance of excessive globalization and standardization is that globalization came to be synonymous with lowest common denominator, global homogenization of marketing.

The Two-Box Model: "Think Globally. Act Locally."

As the late 1990s dawned, there was a perceptual change in how brands viewed the marketing world. Discussions around managing global brands in a more sensitive manner became more prevalent. These discussions focused on how to create, grow, and nurture Brand Strength. Brand Strength includes relevance and differentiation. Organizations realized that as the world became smaller, the intricacies and rewards of localism and regionalism were bigger than originally thought. Inevitably, global marketing moved from the One-Box Standardization Model to the Two-Box Model: "Think globally. Act locally." (TGAL).

"Think globally. Act locally." sounded so appropriate and made such intuitive sense. The initial intentions were valuable and noteworthy. The purpose was to leverage and to be the best of both worlds. Instead of standardized global executions, the "Think globally. Act locally." approach encouraged global thinking executed locally. TGAL quickly became the dominant global marketing mind-set. Yes, marketing strategies and ideas would be globally generated, but the regions now had the opportunity to implement these ideas in locally relevant ways. As John A. Quelch and Katherine E. Jocz pointed out, "By respecting local values and local tastes, by rooting themselves in the community, global brands broaden their appeal and build deeper trust with their consumers."[5]

However, TGAL devolved into just another way for the center to be the controlling leader. Even when the "Think globally. Act locally." approach was activated, the brand vision, brand direction, brand research, brand strategy, and other heavy lifting were to be done by the leadership at the global center. The role of the regions was merely to execute the strategic thoughts of the remote center.

In reality, TGAL became this: "Here in the center, we will do the important thinking globally. Then we will hand it off to the regions to execute our centralized thinking locally." It is a "hand-off model"—a hand-off from the central brains to the regional brawn, where the regions use their marketing muscle to impose centralized thoughts on local audiences. Sadly, TGAL became "Global thinking with regional tinkering." When the headquarters or center was in the United States, "Think globally. Act locally." became "Think USA. Do as we say."

Furthermore, with "Think globally. Act locally." the regions did not have to accept accountability for their actions because all they were doing was carrying out orders. If an idea or a strategy or a plan did not succeed, the regions could say (and did say), "Not my fault; this was not my idea. I am just responsible for executing the center's ideas." And again, with all the important thinking centralized, there was no true catering to local and regional idiosyncrasies or attitudes.

Unfortunately, there was also no accountability at the global center. If an idea or a strategy or a plan did not succeed, the global centralists could say (and did say), "Not my fault; execution is not our responsibility. The local region did a poor job of execution." With a successful implementation, the center would take the credit and fail to appreciate the work the regions had to do to achieve this success. These situations could become quite heated and have lasting consequences if not handled well.

Over time, we learned that the Two-Box Model does not address the tension between global and regional in a manner that best promotes the brand and the organization's talents. This approach became less and less productive as the need for localization increased. It does not leverage the scale of global with the specifics of local. Nor does it fit in with the way the marketing world is developing.

We discussed the rise of personalization. Global brands now must be globally recognizable, coherent, and reliable while also being locally relevant and personally differentiated. Neither the One-Box Model nor the Two-Box Model take into account the powerful intersection of these three forces. A globally standardized One-Box approach paves over the relevancy of local cultures, tastes, desires, and designs and doesn't allow for the intricacies of catering to individuals. The Two-Box approach confuses responsibilities and accountability for results. The center also prefers for its global ideas to remain the same even if these ideas are implemented locally. Our new Model recognizes the imperative for maximizing the power of the three forces. Its structure and clear responsibilities allow for managing against all three in an ordered, disciplined manner. Additionally, our Model is flexible enough to adapt to the most complex matrix management system.

The Matrix

For those who were intrigued by cinema's *The Matrix* trilogy, a civilization with two separate worlds constantly coming into contact—illusionary or not—with one another in master and servant, virtual and real interaction is not so far off from the requirements of modern organizational matrix management. Just as the world is evolving, forcing brands to adopt new ideas and adapt to emerging problematic situations, global marketing has evolved organizationally. As previously discussed, global organizational alignment has its challenges. These are particularly apparent in a global matrix organization (see Figure 6.1).

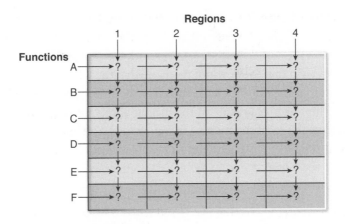

Figure 6.1 Matrix management

Many people feel matrix organizations lack accountability. These structures confuse rather than clarify responsibilities. In some organizations, the "org charts" and the "RACI" charts defining "Who is **R**esponsible, who is **A**ccountable, who is **C**onsulted, and who is **I**nformed" are incomprehensible. Understanding how to manage with these RACI charts usually requires at least one or two workshops with table exercises and multiple presentations, overnight homework, and outside facilitators. RACI charts contribute to ever more confusion.

Yet, matrix management is a marketing fact of life. As complex as it is, matrix management is becoming the current reality because it is the best way to achieve effective collaboration to achieve common goals. Matrix management is a business reality. Sometimes people say they cannot manage what does not report to them. They are uncomfortable managing in a matrix world. Those people who say these things are correct; this is not a situation for them.

Matrix management is difficult and complex. To some it is a hurdle to climbing the corporate ladder. And for others, it is a good place to hide while others fight it out for supremacy. In an organizational setting, the matrix is not an illusion; it is not meant to stymie ambition or stalemate (or even checkmate) decision-making. The matrix is not the problem. How to manage brands in a matrix management world is.

The matrix is designed to array all the interlocking functions into a cohesive, collaborative system that allows for strength in the regions as well as from the center. In the matrix world, the central brand managers often complain that they cannot manage what they do not control. They complain that they do not have the resources to implement their ideas because the resources reside in the local markets. In the center, people do not trust the local capabilities to follow the script. They are right and wrong at the same time. Different organizational functions want to be left to do their own thing, to deliver the deliverables without "interference" from other parts of the organization.

Some people prefer working in a world with clear, linear lines of authority. The matrix world is a challenge for them as well. Matrix management is not hierarchical like Feudalism. The lines of reporting up to a liege lord are not clear because the responsibilities are not always linear. If there is one caveat for dealing with matrix management it is this: beware of overuse of the dotted line. In some companies, to cope with the resentments and risks involved with mastering the matrix, a complex spider web of dotted lines results in a confusing array of connections. If everyone agrees to accountabilities, there is no reason to confuse life with too many dotted lines, which no one understands or can explain.

Management and Manager

From our perspective, after working with many clients that have large branded portfolios, the problems with matrix management begin with a misunderstanding of what it means to manage. Somewhere along the way, the language of business became misused.

Pick a dictionary, whether printed or online, and look up "management." It means to "take charge or take care of...." It means "to handle, to direct, to control the actions." A manager is a person who controls and manipulates resources and expenditures. In global marketing, it is not the person in the center who is the "manager." Why is that? It's because the local store, restaurant, hotel, bank, local franchisee, dealer, sales representative, or service representative is managing the brand experience. Nothing happens until it happens at point of purchase, wherever that point of purchase and service may be. Following this logic, the brand's ultimate responsibility to produce local results must be local. The center's mind-set that it is the global manager is wrong and needs to change. Global, central personnel are not the ultimate managers. They need to be true leaders, and this is a much more difficult task. Brand management is local; brand leadership is global.

Leadership and Leader

"Leadership" is a different role than "manager." It means "to guide or direct." A leader achieves success through passion, persuasion, persistence, conviction, commitment, drive, and diplomacy. Previously, we discussed leadership. A leader inspires, influences, and motivates others. The five pillars of responsibility to lead are inspire, influence, educate, support, and evaluate. This is the role of the center: to be the global leader of the brand.

There is a clear role for central brand leadership for either global organizations or national organizations. It is the leadership responsibility to direct, to guide, to support, to inform, to educate, to facilitate, to influence, to evaluate and learn, and above all to inspire. Leaders succeed through the actions of others whom they influence. A leader's greatest achievements come not by telling the local managers what to do, but by influencing these managers to do the right things in the right way producing the right results. In the matrix system, central leadership and local management are highly balanced between what leadership sees as proper and profitable direction and what managers see as how to achieve success in a locally relevant manner.

When it comes to a global organization, the basic principle to master the matrix—with few exceptions—must be that brand leadership is global while brand management is local. Making the leadership/management separation work properly and actually happen means that job definitions will change. We have worked with a variety of clients on marketing handbooks. These handbooks usually move along smoothly until the section on job descriptions. With one client, the final version of the marketing handbook was number 72—72 versions editing and reediting due to discomfort with the job description section. People do not want to give up anything; no activity is too small to risk losing. And they often do not want their job to be modified. It is common to hear things like, "*They* are not doing the right things in the right way. But, *I* am doing just fine."

Putting the Right People in the Right Places

Remember the earlier discussion about putting the right people on the right bus? Changing the mind-set also means making sure that "you have the right people on the right bus in the right seats."[6] Not everyone is a leader or wants to be in a leadership position; some people prefer "line" roles and responsibilities. Others serve the brand and the organization better by moving to a central, leadership position. HR has a huge role to play in ensuring that people with the right skillsets and the right ambitions and attitudes are in the correct matrix positions. However, the responsibility of HR is to make the understanding of roles and responsibilities an easy task. In many cases, HR makes mastering the matrix an endless brain-numbing series of workshops and seminars with 3-inch binders and exercises and videos and web-based training. This does not rally the teams around the new way of working; it bores the teams into submission.

Results Are Local

By far, the biggest matrix mind-set shift is recognizing that because results are created locally, the local marketing teams have primary accountability for results. Therefore, the local marketers must also have responsibility for being regional thought leaders, not just mere implementers of the ideas of remote, central big thinkers. YUM! Brands such as Pizza Hut and KFC are excellent examples of regional empowerment. In China, the local management has been empowered to evolve these brands in ways that are relevant to the local needs and opportunities. Over the years this has been an amazing success story for YUM! Brands.

Global Brand Leadership acts as a global brand ambassador using the powers of education, thought leadership, inspiration, and persuasion to achieve consistency. However, within a clear framework, the regional and local teams need to be given the freedom to create and implement what they see as necessary for the enduring profitable success of the brand in their territories. The Collaborative Three-Box Model rests on achieving the proper balance of these responsibilities.

Responsibility: Global or Local

The big question that we are frequently asked is this: Is the responsibility for results global or local? Our answer is, "Yes." The new imperative is *shared responsibility*. Today, cocreative, cooperative, collaborative, shared responsibilities are transforming the way we live and work. Sharing responsibility is just as critical a factor when you are an organizational sharer. Sharing is already a business basic, not just a socializing necessity: "The spread of mobile devices is forcing changes in the ways workers communicate and share information. Mobile access is expected. Communication between groups of employees has become far more open while collaboration around work happens instantly."[7]

Matrix management relies on shared responsibilities across geographies. This means that there will be people who have multiple leaders through dotted lines of reporting. There will also be leaders who "share" personnel through dotted-line reporting. For example, a global research director will have a team of central, direct reports. However, the regional research leaders will report to the global leader only by dotted line because their real responsibility is to the regional president.

Sharing

Unfortunately, language and meaning are once again obstacles. Sharing responsibilities in some organizations has mutated into partitioning responsibilities. In mastering the matrix, partitioning is about separation, not sharing. "You do your thing. I will do mine." Partitioning and partnership have little in common. Partitioning is what leads to the "silo" mentality. Partitioning is about dividing powers into parts where each owner of a part manages that particular piece without the constraints of the other part owners. It is similar to renting a house to a group of individuals in a summer vacation area: all the food in the refrigerator is designated by a person's name. Each owner separates her food even though everyone shares the house and the refrigerator. Partitioning is a shoji screen: the shoji screen is the defense against encroachment.

ew is that instead of a "hand-off" model of partitioned responsibilities, mastering the matrix needs to evolve toward a model of shared responsibilities. This new emphasis on shared responsibilities is very different.

Sharing is the new essential.[8] Today, the way we work together better will be through cocreative, cooperative, coordinated, collaborative, shared responsibilities. Shared responsibility for effective global brand building is not easy to accomplish.

The Collaborative Three-Box Model

The new emphasis on shared responsibilities is already having significant impact on how we approach global brand management. It leads us to our third approach, what we call The Collaborative Three-Box Model.

As we discuss in the following chapters, The Collaborative Three-Box Model has three phases:

1. Create the brand vision.

2. Define the global brand plan to win.

3. Bring the brand to life.

Figure 6.2 The Collaborative Three-Box Model

With a truly shared responsibility model, the coordination, cooperation, collaboration, and collective responsibilities change the way we think and the way we work together to achieve our common ambitions.

Collaboration is so much more effective than confrontation. It is also much more effective than the isolation of the silo mentality—the "Let me do my thing my way" approach. In one instance, a small regional agency developed a creative idea. It was agreed that this idea had great global potential. But a lead creative director at the headquarters agency quit the agency instead of adopting and adapting an idea from the small satellite agency in his own network of agencies.

There are advantages to global marketing, just as there are advantages to localized marketing and personalized marketing. However, bland, undifferentiated, centralized-only thinking of the marketing landscape destroys these advantages. Viewing the world as monolithic is myopic. Globalization now shares the stage with localization and personalization. Finding the best way in which to manage the matrix while building and nurturing brands across geographies and functions is a key factor in twenty-first century business success. Shared responsibility works better than partitioned responsibility.

As a result of our varied experiences on the client side, on the agency side, and as consultants, we developed this new method as the best approach to brand building either nationwide or worldwide. The splintering and fractionalization that results from the growth of individuality will continue. Yet there are still those stalwarts of standardization who continue to believe in the lowest common denominator of the marketplace. They believe that homogenized, mass marketing is the future. These crusaders of commonality continue to believe that the marketing world is becoming more monolithic. These proponents of a uniform, smoothed-over world ignore the inexorable trends of increased segmentation and fragmentation. They insist that we should think of the world as unvarying, indivisible blocks with everyone wanting the same mass brand served to them in the same mass way. A monolithic marketing mind-set is a mistaken message for today's multicultural, multifaceted, multisegmented, multidimensional world.

Market segmentation, localism, nationalization, self-sorting, personalization, and customization are not the future. They are here and happening today. As we pointed out in the *Journal of Brand Strategy* in 2013:

"...in 1999, Jose Bove, an agricultural unionist, became a hero to anti-globalization supporters when he and his political group, Confederation Paysanne, bulldozed a McDonald's in Milau, France. Yet today, France is McDonald's second-most profitable market in the world. The chain has more than 1,200 restaurants in France—all locally owned franchises. What is at the heart of this impressive performance that has stunned French observers and surprised business analysts? The main reason for McDonald's success is the localization of the global brand." For example, the McDonald's local menu included items like a le McBaguette sandwich of excellent ham, and French cheese on a crispy baguette.

"In many companies, the going-in premise is that China is different. The IHG China team agreed that while the Crowne Plaza brand is in a very different place from the USA, Crowne Plaza shares the same brand ambition and brand framework around the world. The China team created a great marketing campaign within the global framework. The result was a 7-percentage point increase in brand consideration and a 4-percentage point increase in brand preference all within two months."[9]

The Kinship Economy

Our global world is fast becoming a whole of many parts, and the opportunities for marketing are extraordinary. In its 2013 Trends Report, *The Kinship Economy*, IHG identified several significant paradoxes. One of these is the paradox of global hospitality brands needing to satisfy the "multidimensional" needs of travelers as a result of shifts in demography and lifestyles. The *IHG Trends Report* points out that, "There is also increasing demand for personalized and customized service—people want to feel special."[10] Not only are there many different types of travelers with different needs, these individual travelers will have different needs over the course of a single trip.

Guided Decentralization

The Collaborative Three-Box Model addresses this important paradox of marketing. This Model is not a centralized dictatorship, nor is it a two-step, partitioned TGAL hand-off of responsibilities. It is not just a process change; as we emphasized, it is a mind-set change, a cultural change, an organizational change. It means mastering the matrix. It is neither decentralization nor centralization; it is guided decentralization with leadership emanating from the center but with management of results located in the regions. It is global harmonization; everyone may have different parts to sing, but when the audience hears the output, it is symphonic and pleasantly melodious.

Is It Federalism?

As long ago as 1996, Charles Handy wrote eloquently about some paradoxes of business. One was the fact that organizations need to be big and small at the same time. They need the economy of scale. They also need the resources to fund innovations and renovations. Bigness, he said, is necessary to make an organization less dependent on a small number of people internally or externally and less dependent on outside consultancies. But organizations must also be small. Smaller entities want autonomy; people are identifying with communities and cultures and groups. Small is comfortable, flexible, and more likely to be creative and innovative. Handy suggested federalism. But in his mind, the center was not a bank just funding the regions. Nor were the regions separate entities. "Federalism responds to all these pressures, balancing power among those in the center of the organization, those in the center of expertise, and those in the center of the action, the operating businesses."[11]

The Collaborative Three-Box Model adapts some of this approach but adds the discipline and process for day-to-day operations as well as being a model of mastering the matrix for building powerful global brands. This is not easy. But it has to happen because our world's changes are creating a place that demands this particular type of shepherded separation under the brand banner. The winners will be the ones that build great global brands that are locally relevant and personally differentiated. The shared responsibility Model provides marketing muscle so organizations can have brand strength and power to compete both effectively and efficiently.

Endnotes

1. Harrison, George, "Any Road," *Brainwashed*, released posthumously May 12, 2003.

2. For our detailed discussion of this evolution see Light, Larry, "How Organizations Manage Brands in an Increasingly Global World," *Journal of Brand Strategy*, Vol. 2, No. 3, Summer 2013, pp. 228–235.

3. Levitt, Theodore, "The Globalization of Marketing," *Harvard Business Review*, May/June, 1983.

4. Levitt, Theodore, "The Globalization of Marketing," *McKinsey Quarterly*, Summer, 1994.

5. Quelch, John A. and Jocz, Katherine E., *All Business Is Local: Why Place Matters More Than Ever in a Global, Virtual World*, Penguin Business, UK, 2012, p 21.

6. Collins, Jim, *Good to Great: How Some Companies Make the Leap...and Others Don't*, Harper Collins, 2001.

7. Waters, Richard and Kuchler, Hannah, "Social Networks Now a Staple of Office Life: Facebook Seeks to Take Advantage of the Changing Ways in Which Workers Communicate and Share Information," *Financial Times*, November 19, 2014.

8. *The Economist*, Leaders column, March 9, 2013.

9. Light, Larry, "How Organizations Manage Brands in an Increasingly Global World," *Journal of Brand Strategy*, Vol. 2, No. 3, Summer 2013, pp. 228–235.

10. *The New Kinship Economy: From Travel Experiences to Travel Relationships*, IHG, February 2013.

11. Handy, Charles, *Beyond Certainty: The Changing Worlds of Organizations*, Harvard Business School Press, MA, 1996, pp. 36–37.

7

The Collaborative Three-Box Model: Box 1—Create the Brand Vision

Looking for directions
Stars are your reflections

—U2, North Star[1]

In real estate, the mantra is "location, location, location." In The Collaborative Three-Box Model, the Box 1 mantra is "direction, direction, direction." The first step is the definition of the brand's North Star. Every brand needs clear direction; every brand needs a vision of what it wants to be and where it wants to go.

Begin with the Corporate Strategies and Ambition

Beginning the process does not mean starting with a blank piece of paper. Most companies and brands have lots of information. This information sets up the context for this new global marketing approach.

There are many places to look for providing the context for The Model. It must be nested within the articulated corporate direction. For example, corporate strategies and other priorities are often reflected in reports, presentations, interviews, and articles, including statements of the corporate history, vision, mission, and values. A brand does not operate in a vacuum; it works under the influence of the corporate culture and strategy.

Cross-Functional Teams (CFTs)

We have mentioned the need for cross-functional teams (CFTs) several times. If you want to break down silos and make the matrix system manageable, you need to institute CFTs. Although it's difficult to do, clients who have gone through the process say that the CFT was their best business learning experience.

Putting The Model into play means creating a dedicated cross-functional (CFT), cross-geographic team and insisting on full participation. Calendar management will be one of the main hurdles in making the CFT happen. Sometimes the nonenthusiasts use their busy calendars as excuses for not participating. Attendance and participation in cross-functional meetings is not an option. The CEO must reinforce this behavioral commitment for perfect attendance.

Box 1: Defining the Brand North Star

In The Collaborative Three-Box Model, Box 1 defines the brand's North Star, the brand's common Ambition. Each company will have its own term for this overarching definition of where it wants the brand to be and what it wants the brand to achieve. Use whichever definition makes the most sense internally. We define the common Ambition as the description of what the brand can and should aim to become on its journey to greatness.

Creating the Brand Ambition is not just a forecast extrapolated from how we are perceived and positioned today. Brand Ambition is an inspiring definition of where we believe the brand can and should be. There will be a gap between today and tomorrow. That's good. There needs to be a gap between where we are and where we wish to be. The challenge is to close the gap. Where we want our brand to be answers these questions:

- What mind-space do we want to dominate?
- As we look down the road, how do we define brand success?

The Brand Ambition should be a vision of perfection. As Toyota says for Lexus, it is a relentless pursuit. We will never reach perfection, but we should always aim for it. Why aim for anything less? Instead of asking, "Are we there, yet?" we should ask, "Are we making meaningful progress?"

Defining the Brand Ambition is a shared responsibility. The Global Brand Leadership leads this effort. The responsibility for Box 1 is 80% global and 20% regional. Yet, there must be essential collaborative input from a cross-functional, cross-geographic team of regional brand leaders and functional leaders. It is the task of Global Brand Leadership to synthesize the input of the cross-functional, cross-geographic team discussions into a compelling, coherent statement of the Brand Ambition.

Writing a Brand Ambition requires expertise, knowledge, and judgment. Creating this guiding visionary statement requires confidence and the ability to take a leap of faith. It means understanding when the gap between where we are now and where we want to be is a possible dream or an impossible dream. One of the goals of the CFT is to think about closing the gap as a major brand challenge. How we plan to close the gap is the brand's roadmap for the future: what do we need to do to make progress toward our brand North Star?

The Four Steps of Box 1

Box 1 has four main components (see Figure 7.1):

1. Situation analysis
2. Trends
3. Market segmentation
4. Brand Ambition

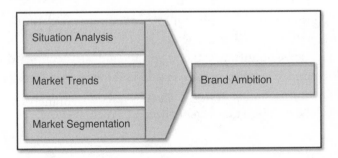

Figure 7.1 Three-Box Model: Box 1

Again, each organization may have different terms for these four elements. Use whatever language works best in your corporate and brand context. But please remember that whatever language is used, it must be consistent worldwide. The underlying thought of The Collaborative Three-Box Model is consistency and discipline. These four "buckets" reflect the important categories that must be covered to understand where the brand is now and help spark thinking about where we want the brand to be. After these four areas are complete, the Global Brand Leadership will prepare a common Ambition statement that will be used as the overarching direction for Box 2 and Box 3.

1. Situation Analysis

This section is essentially a platform defining the brand's current business environment. Additionally, this section is used to highlight current knowledge about the brand's capabilities. To win in tomorrow's world, it is essential to know where the brand is now in today's business marketplace. What are the environmental dynamics that are affecting the brand, positively and negatively?

This is no small task for the Global Brand Leadership team. Information exists in all the countries in which the brand does business. Besides data and written reports, a lot of information resides with individuals who have experience with the brand. Even though it is the responsibility of the Global Brand Leadership team to create the situation analysis, they must respect the input of their functional and regional partners. The brand-focused discussions must be open and frank. The final document must be a reflection of all the issues, whether global, regional, or local.

Types of Information Needed

Each function and geography will be asked to provide information for the situation analysis. All the needed information should be cross-functional, cross-industry, within a specific industry, competitive, and brand focused. The information should be broad based. This is about the global brand on an overarching macro level, not how the global brand will be localized and personalized at a regional level.

The information should cover topics such as these:[2]

- Business situation, priorities, and constraints
- Priority countries, areas, regions
- Demographics: age, gender, employment, population growth estimates, and so on
- All marketplace conditions including social, economic, political, environmental, and industry landscapes
- Brand ratings, rankings, insights, and performance relative to competition
- Competitor information globally and by country
- Competitor annual reports, CEO speeches, PR, and so on
- All other relevant brand diagnostics
- Technology, digital, virtual, mobile, social networking changes, and innovations
- Media
- Regulatory issues including environmental
- Any other business, marketing, social, political forces that may be or currently are affecting the brand or one or more competitors

Questions to Ask within the CFT

Team members should ask themselves a variety of basic brand questions such as these:

- What are the brand's priorities?
- What is the relevant market structure?
- What are the key marketplace challenges?
- What is the brand's performance? How is the brand performing relative to a customer-perceived competitive set?
- What is the brand's image?
- What are the gaps between the brand's reality and its perceptions?
- What specific issues does the brand need to address?

- What is the brand's customer-perceived value?
- Which drivers of brand value are strongest? Which drivers of brand value are weakest?
- What are the relevant metrics for defining success?

The global brand leadership is responsible for guiding the situation analysis process. It is the role of global leadership to synthesize all information into a usable, action-oriented document. This knowledge-based document will provide clarity and steer decision-making.

SWOTTA

For a situation analysis, many organizations use a format known as SWOT: strengths, weaknesses, opportunities, and threats. We recommend a global brand SWOTTA that includes trends and actions (see Figure 7.2). SWOTTA stands for strengths, weaknesses, opportunities, trends, threats, and actions. SWOTTA is not merely a descriptive document. It is action oriented.

	People	Product	Place	Price	Promotion
Strengths					
Weaknesses					
Opportunities					
Trends					
Threats					
Actions					

Figure 7.2 SWOTTA

The SWOTTA reflects all the information from Box 1. An important part of Box 1 is identifying and understanding the impact of trends if brand relevance is to be maintained. In the final SWOTTA document, trends merit special attention. Brand management is not about defending the past. It is about managing the future.

It is vital that the SWOTTA highlight the actions that will drive measurable results leading to the sustainable profitable growth of the brand. If there are no actions, Box 1 becomes academic and theoretical. Without actions, Box 1 is nice to have, but everyone will go right back to business as usual. So it is necessary to highlight both the relevant trends and the specific actions that will drive the brand's growth. The SWOTTA analysis must be explicit about the action implications. A proper SWOTTA ties strengths, weaknesses, opportunities, trends, threats, and actions to each of the five Action Ps (people, product/service, place, price, promotion) in the brand's Plan to Win. In Chapter 11, "How Does It All Come Together in an Effective Plan to Win?," we discuss the Plan to Win in detail. The resulting SWOTTA from Box 1 will be a 6 × 5 matrix.

2. Trends

There are two types of trends. There are the data-based trends: these include demographics, including all population changes and forecasts; competitive developments; attitudinal and behavioral changes; business trends; technological trends; mobile, digital, social networking trends; diet; health; and so forth. Then there is the creative synthesis trend where ideas come from, seeking patterns within data, news, events, stories, histories, and more.

It is not sufficient to just look at quantification through analytics. This is a good start, but it will not lead to real competitive advantage. What are the root causes of the trends? What are their implications? Oil prices are falling. What are the implications for fast food?

Analytic trends tend to be a commodity—anyone can find and report on this data. Analytic trends are based on the information that is available. Reporting is good. Competitors have the same information that you have. You need analytic trends, but these do not provide profound, differential insight.

Trends based on synthesis offer added value to the context in which brands operate and help us draw conclusions for possible future scenarios. Synthesis derives from looking at the information and learning and then seeing patterns beneath the surface. Synthesis offers insights that are more than just reporting or observation. True actionable insights deliver against three criteria, in this order (see Figure 7.3):

1. **Surprise at what is learned**—"WOW, I did not know that."
2. **Learning that is brand relevant**—"It is important because..."
3. **What actions will I implement?**—"Based on what I now know, here is what I will have to do differently."[3]

I did not know that...	
This is important because...	
This is what we will have to do differently...	

Figure 7.3 Actionable insight

Analyses of data that create trends come from breaking down and examining numerical information and reporting on how the data move across time. Synthesis comes from interpreting data, integrating data with other ideas, and combining qualitative and quantitative information. Analysis takes things apart and describes what is happening. Synthesis puts things together in original ways and sees what others fail to see. Synthesis is the basis for developing meaningful, actionable, true insight.

> "Creativity is just connecting things. When you ask creative people how they did something, they feel a little guilty, because they didn't really do it, they just saw something. It seemed obvious to them after a while. That's because they were able to connect experiences they've had and synthesize new things."[4]

Professor Howard Gardner of Harvard wrote about people who can synthesize. He was looking at what kinds of people organizations should hire in the future. He identified five types of minds. The Synthesizing Mind is the ability to select critical information from all the available information and then array that information in ways that make sense. He said,

> "The ability to knit together information from disparate sources into a coherent whole is vital today. The amount of accumulated knowledge is reportedly doubling every two to three years (wisdom presumably accrues more slowly!). Sources of information are vast and disparate, and individuals crave coherence and integration. Nobel Prize-winning physicist Murray Gell-Mann has asserted that the mind most at premium in the twenty-first century will be the mind that can synthesize well."[5]

We provide an example of an insight template (see Figure 7.4). Although this example seems so normal now, imagine it were 10 years ago. At that time, beverages were meal accompaniments and not meals in themselves. Jamba Juice had just started to grow. And juicing was neither a habit nor a verb.

I did not know that...	A convenient, portable beverage can be a tasty, healthful meal for both adults and kids.
This is important because...	Both adults and children are not getting the proper daily nutrition.
This is what we will have to do differently...	Create a line of balanced, nutritious, portable beverages that are not meal accompaniments but meals in themselves

Figure 7.4 Actionable insight example

3. Market Segmentation

The role of marketing is to profitably provide branded products and services to satisfy customer wants at superior customer-perceived brand value compared to competitive alternatives. Identifying and understanding the priority customers is the purpose of market segmentation.

Market segmentation addresses several key areas helping to direct brand-business strategy and brand policy and drive resource allocation. It offers us the following:

- Superior understanding of the customer so the brand can provide outstanding competitive advantage
- Strategic focus that is fundamental to effective marketing
- Identifying market priorities; effective market segmentation drives business strategy, not just brand strategy[6]

This means defining the following:

- Who are the prime customers and prospects?
- What are their needs and problems?
- What are the occasions in which these needs occur?

A market segment is a specific group of people with common values who share common needs in a common context. Product categories, channels, or price categories are not market segments; there is no such thing as the mobile phone market, no such thing as the fresh-pressed juice market, no such thing as the granola bar market. There is a market for portable, quick, easy-to-use and stylish networked communications. There is a market for an afternoon revitalizer. There is a market for a healthy, attractive fit body. A market is not a product; it is a need. If there is no need, there is no market. If it is a growing need, it is a growing market. If it is a global need, it is a global market.

Knowing the audience, knowing the need, and knowing the occasion are all important. The challenge is to combine these three into a brand-focused, complete market segment. This three-dimensional view of the market is foundational. The real work of segmentation is creating a clear and understandable market definition based on who the audience is, what this audience needs that the product/service will satisfy, and what the occasion is for which this audience has this need. The final output is a synthesized brand portrait that articulates the essential characteristics differentiating a brand's target market segment.

"Market segmentation is an essential element of marketing. Goods can no longer be produced and sold without considering the customer needs and recognizing the heterogeneity of those needs."[7]

4. SMART Objectives

After the first three elements of Box 1 are gathered, discussed, debated, and decided, it is the role of the Global Brand Leadership to achieve agreement to the Brand Ambition and the SMART Objectives for the brand.

SMART Objectives describe the measurable goals that need to be met to achieve the vision. These metrics must be consistent over time, across businesses, and across geography. The SMART Objectives have the following characteristics:

- Specific
- Measurable
- Aspirational yet achievable
- Related to overall business growth
- Time specific

Brand Ambition Template

As we mentioned earlier, the Brand Ambition is the statement of where you want the brand to be in the future (see Figure 7.5). It is composed of answers to three thoughts:

1. I see a world in which brand X...
2. In order for this to happen...
3. Brand X will...

These three answers need to be combined into a cogent and compelling thought (see Figure 7.6).

I see a world in which…	
In order for this to happen…	
Our brand will…	

Figure 7.5 Brand Ambition template

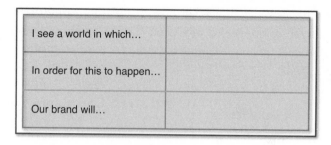

Figure 7.6 Brand Ambition example

Brand Ambition Statement

The final Brand Ambition statement should be competitive. Why will this brand be superior to competitive alternatives? There are three ways to be a superior choice:

1. Do what competitors do but do it better.

2. Do something relevant that competitors do not do.

3. Do what others do but do it at lower cost to the customer.

Making Box 1 Work

1. Make It Everyone's Job to Take Responsibility

We say responsibility in Box 1 is divided 80% global and 20% local. However, as we described earlier, leadership is about coaxing, not commanding. Global Brand Leadership must be responsible because this box is about setting the agenda for the brand's consistent core as it crosses geography. It is the overarching description of the brand's priority market segment. It defines the brand core that will underpin the experience it will deliver and defines the global Brand Ambition. It includes the common SMART objectives. The regional teams and functions must participate and not sit by idly. What happens in Box 1 affects the next two boxes. Ultimately, the Global team is responsible for developing the integrated pan-geography view of the brand vision. But that does not mean that regional personnel abdicate their responsibility to express their views and contribute. No decisions or actions at any point in The Collaborative Three-Box Model are solo performances. Box 1 is the opening act for collaboration. If it does not work here, it will not work down the line.

2. Make Sure That Your CFT and Your Enterprise Become a Learning Organization

Sharing of global learning saves resources and empowers multiple countries. Hoarding information is unproductive. When information is shared, there is a return on that learning. Sharing is happening all around us, yet in many companies information stays locked in someone's file on his computer, sometimes never to see the light of day again. This hoarding of information is related to "who owns the information?" The company owns the information, not a person. It is in the best interest of all that information be shared with everyone.

3. Stay Positive When the Killer Questions Are Raised About Your Synthesized Trends

Some examples of killer questions are, "Are you certain this idea will succeed?" "Have you measured it?" "Can you prove it?" "Who else has done this?" Synthesized trends are about the future. The goal is actionable insights leading to new creative ideas that result in competitive advantage. If others are already doing them, then the ideas are not new. There is always going to be something that we do not know; something that we are not certain about. Synthesis is not guesswork. It is action based on informed judgment combined with expertise.

Although we cannot measure the ideas themselves, we can create concepts and prototypes to obtain insight into customer reactions to the ideas. We can only measure what we can measure. And, as Einstein said, "Not everything we can measure matters. And not everything that matters can be measured." We are never certain about the future. But based on judgment, information, and expertise, we can be confident that the creative synthesis reflects our best thinking.

4. Ensure That the Situation Analysis Will Be Updated Each Year

The world is changing so quickly. New ideas and competitors arrive and leave. Technology is spurring all sorts of new ways to live and connect. People, especially young people, are able to adapt swiftly. It is always good to be ahead of the game. Some updates will be small; some will be not so small. Once the SWOTTA is developed, it is easier to update.

5. Market Segmentation Is a Market Fundamental

Be a market segmentation advocate. But also make it your mission that segmentation be *one* of the tools in the toolbox, *not the only tool*. Some view segmentation as the answer to every question. This is a mistake. Segmentation often raises more questions than it answers. Segmentation works well with other market research. It is the basis of a lot of corporate and brand strategies. The segments that are created can become the screeners for other studies. It is a gold mine for data mining. At one client, we mined the data for 3 years. However, at some point, the segmentation data will need to be refreshed. Even though segmentation may uncover or explain universal needs, in a volatile changing world, it is essential to keep the information fresh. Nothing should ever be bronzed. Consider conducting segmentation every 3–5 years.

Lessons Learned: Box 1

Lesson One: Avoid the Wholesale Importing of Concepts with No Adaptation

We learned from years of global observation that it is often best to "adopt, adapt, and scale" good ideas. Good ideas do not care where they come from. However, a completely standardized, inflexible idea with no "adaptation" can be a bad way to do business. Walmart took this approach with its stores in Germany. Soon, it had to sell to Metro because the USA way failed. Carrefour ran into trouble importing its French concept in South America. Tesco tried to import the European-style neighborhood, small space market into America's western states and failed to understand just how little Americans found that appealing. It only took five agonizing years before *Fresh and Easy* folded in 2013.

Good ideas can be spread around the world; just make sure these ideas are adapted to the cultural and social idiosyncrasies of the locale. Adaptation may be needed to institutionalize a new idea worldwide. As with Freedom within a Framework, as long as the core idea is kept alive, how the idea is made relevant locally will be fine. Let's say you run a restaurant chain that has a buffet with a signature item. That signature item need not be the same in each country. Is a Happy Meal less than a Happy Meal if the varieties of beverages offered vary by country?

Lesson Two: Avoid Analysis Paralysis

Data can anesthetize the mind, especially in today's information age. Just because there are research, statistics, and other data to understand and use does not mean that the CFT should become incapable of moving forward. Numbers can generate numbness, but this is mainly because people expect the research rather than the researchers to provide real answers. There must be a going-in rule that the role of research is to inform you rather than make the decisions for you. Researchers will always want to do more research to help you find the answers. Research provides direction and raises questions, but please remember that data does not think or speak; people do. Make sure that your researchers are helping the team move forward rather than hindering progress. Our experience is that once people understand that the data does not decide, they feel liberated and creative.

Before automatically initiating a large, new research project, derive insight from the research you already have. Years ago, we worked with a client on a large-scale, multiple brands research study. We were the "coordinator" of the various brand teams and their three respective advertising agencies—meaning three different agency research departments. After weeks of presentations and meetings, the clients selected the one vendor who would conduct the research. Many months later, at the unveiling of the results, the research vendor spent three hours reciting the findings from five large FedEx boxes of charts, drawing not one insightful conclusion. Without any direction from the research, the client felt stymied. It became our job to "Please tell us what all this means."

More recently, we attended a research meeting where a well-known advertising testing company showed that the client's advertising was having a negative impact on the brand because the campaign confused customers. There was no action list after the presentation: no to-do list or stop-do list. Nothing. The presenter was inert in terms of any potential actions. He was reluctant to provide any answer to, "So, what do you recommend we do about this?" Finally, after a lot of pressure, the presenter finally said, "Put more money into advertising." Really? More money behind a campaign that is already confusing people will just confuse more people. Research does not make decisions; it informs decisions. Interpret what you learn. Synthesize the information with what you know. It is the fuel for your creative engine. Ask, "What do I do with this information?"

Lesson Three: Use Occasion-Based Needs Segmentation as a Brand-Building Tool

Without meaningful market segmentation, a brand's focus is to "be all things to all people." You have heard branders say, "We have a big brand; we have to appeal to everyone." With this attitude, your brand is acceptable to many and preferred by just a few. Turn "all things to all people" into "great things for some people." This means truly understanding the needs and the occasions for your brand. It means selecting the desired target audiences who have these needs and these occasions. It means learning how to say "no" to a segment. We encounter the "I want it all" syndrome with clients in all industries. Recently, a client's study identified seven segments for the brand and decided to provide offerings for all seven, with the attitude, "Why leave anyone out?" The answer is that by going after seven segments, the brand becomes unfocused. It will not matter how great your promise is and how fantastic your research is; not having focus is detrimental to brand health. In another instance, after spending a year on global segmentation research with a detailed understanding of needs and occasions, a client's corporate strategy department still had to force the segments into price points so it would be easier to understand, technically defeating the purpose behind conducting the research in the first place. Pricing can be so enticing for those who do not want to really think about the world from the customer's perspective. It is the confusion between price and value that causes these strategic mistakes.

Here's one more issue with occasion-based needs segmentation. Many times, in a CFT, a particular country will insist that it is different and that a global world view of needs is wrong for it. Collaboration can help, but it can go only so far. Global segmentation uncovers universal needs that by definition apply everywhere. It is then the country's responsibility to address these needs regionally or locally. We have worked with clients who have generated segmentations by conducting a global study and with clients who have conducted local segmentation studies and built a global one from the results. Either way, the consistency of needs is striking. The globally run studies show the same universal segments country to country. The locally run studies show the same universal segments country to country. This seems to apply regardless of where the country sits on the developing to developed spectrum. It is how these brands are brought to life on the ground in a country where the differences country to country need to be addressed.

Endnotes

1. U2, "North Star," never released but played at the U2 360 concert.

2. For decades, we have asked clients to prepare this list of information as a foundation for a "desk-top" review. The situation analysis begins essentially with a global/regional/local desk-top review.

3. See our discussion about synthesis in Light, Larry and Kiddon, Joan, *The Six Rules of Brand Revitalization: Learn How Companies Like McDonald's Can Re-Energize Their Brands*, Wharton School Publishing, Pearson Education Inc., NJ, 2009, pp. 71–73.

4. Steve Jobs as quoted in Pentland, Alex, *Social Physics: How Good Ideas Spread—The Lessons from a New Science*, The Penguin Press, NY, 2014, p. 26.

5. Gardner, Howard, *Five Minds for the Future*, Harvard Business School Press, MA, 2007, p. 46.

6. For a deep discussion on market segmentation, please see Light, Larry and Kiddon, Joan, *The Six Rules of Brand Revitalization: Learn How Companies Like McDonald's Can Re-Energize Their Brands*, Wharton School Publishing, Pearson Education Inc., NJ, 2009, pp. 61–71.

7. Wedel, Michael and Kamakura, Wagner, *Market Segmentation: Conceptual and Methodological Foundations*, 2nd Edition, Kluwer Academic Publishers, MA, 2000, p. 3.

8

The Collaborative Three-Box Model: Box 2—Define the Global Brand Plan to Win

Down the Rock Island Line, she's a mighty good road
Rock Island Line, it's the road to ride
Rock Island Line, it's a mighty good road
Well if you ride it, you got to ride it, like you find it
Get your ticket at the station for the Rock Island Line[1]

—Songwriter unknown

On May 10, 1869, the "Golden Spike" opened the first U.S. transcontinental railroad linking Council Bluffs, Iowa, with San Francisco, California. Three private companies worked on three separate sections, now all connected. This opened the Western part of the country to more trade and the gold mines of Sutter's Mill. Although every company "won" getting to this spectacular moment, the country won as well. Of course, it was not easy. Egos, competitiveness, labor, and weather all created issues that were difficult to diffuse. Yet, in the end, it worked. Having those routes linked was more important than having anything else.

The Collaborative Three-Box Model has some similarities to this railroad venture. It is not easy, egos get in the way, and people can be at each other's throats from time to time. But it is worth it for the participants, the brand, and the brand's customers and potential customers.

In Box 1, the responsibilities are 80% global and 20% regional, but total participation is a responsibility for every participant. Box 2 is much more challenging; people have to meet halfway but not in a half-hearted manner. Box 2 is a much more difficult stage because responsibility is allocated 50% global and 50% regional. This is not easy; it requires a genuine commitment to real collaboration.

The Global Brand Leadership "owns" the outcome of Box 2. But this ownership is based on the decision-making input of equals. Global team leaders do not dominate the decision-making, and neither does local management.

There are two major outputs of Box 2: The Global Brand Framework and the Global Brand Plan to Win (see Figure 8.1). Although the processes and the development of the Brand Framework and the Global Brand Plan to Win are shared, once completed, it is Global Brand Leadership's responsibility to maintain the Framework's integrity around the world and across functions. This is something similar to a UN or NATO peacekeeping force.

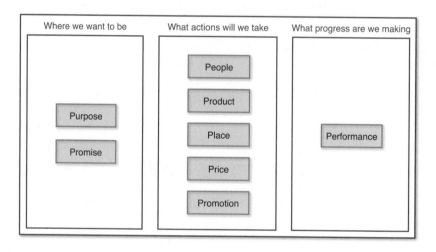

Figure 8.1 Brand Plan to Win

In our experience, as far back as 1990, Mars implemented a global system that did an excellent job of developing, evolving, and maintaining Global Brand Frameworks. Each brand had a cross-functional, cross-geography team that met several times a year to review activities (including innovations, renovations, ingredients, media, and so on) around the brand relative to the Framework. Is what you are doing within the Framework or not? Changes or activities that were deemed outside the Brand Framework were stopped. A Brand Strategic Leader (BSL) led the Framework meetings. The entire organization of Mars associates was committed to the BSL/Brand Framework system.

Box 2 has six components (see Figure 8.2):

1. Brand Pyramid
2. Brand Promise
3. Brand Essence and Guiding Principles
4. Brand Framework
5. Brand Book
6. Global Brand Plan to Win

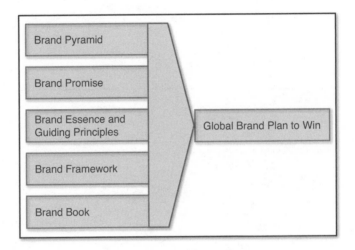

Figure 8.2 Three-Box Model: Box 2

1. Brand Pyramid[2]

The Brand Pyramid is a graphic tool for identifying the relevant and differentiating elements of the brand (see Figure 8.3). It is a sequenced approach to thinking about what we want the brand to be in the customer's mind. The Brand Pyramid identifies the specific relevance and differentiation of the brand experience that will be summarized in the Brand Promise (statement).

The Brand Pyramid consists of the five levels of the brand's relevant differentiation as follows (see Figure 8.4):

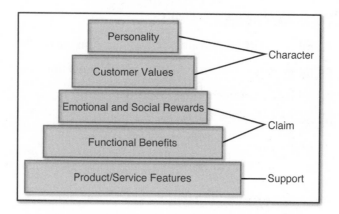

Figure 8.3 Brand Pyramid

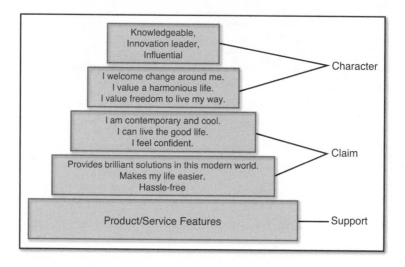

Figure 8.4 Brand Pyramid—example

- The Brand Claim
    - Functional benefits—What the brand does for me
    - Emotional benefits—How that makes me feel
    - Social benefits—How does this brand make me look to myself and others; how does it help me connect to others; do I feel this brand is socially responsible

- The Brand Character
    - Values—The brand values that distinguish the target audience
    - Personality—The distinguishing human qualities that that the target audience will find most appealing
- The Brand Support
    - The key product and service features that make the brand claim credible.

The Brand Pyramid process is a collaborative effort and a creative process. It takes crafting. The CFT works together to build the articulation of the brand's features, functional benefits, emotional and social benefits, customer values, and brand personality. This is created using brand research and marketplace observation as well as the expertise, experience, insight, and judgment of the CFT members.

Although it may seem that this is just a "fill in the blanks" exercise, it is not. Building a Brand Pyramid is a workshop activity. The Global Brand Leadership runs the session. This workshop is a total immersion into the brand and its target audience. The process is collaborative and challenging and difficult to accomplish without a segmentation scheme. The thought process is based on knowing who the intended target is and what the target's needs and occasions are.

Building the Brand Pyramid is the important first step for Box 2. Without the Brand Pyramid, you will not have the foundation for understanding the brand in a consistent manner across geography and across function.

How to Create a Brand Pyramid

To create the Brand Pyramid, start with both qualitative and quantitative interviews with prime customers and prime prospects. This should be available from the information gathered in Box 1.

Who are the customers you have, and who are the prospects you want to have? Everyone, global or regional, has a particular prospect in mind that represents the brand's target customer. The challenge is to achieve global agreement about the key target differentiators that will resonate worldwide. There may be differences by region, but that is acceptable. Not every country is in the same stage of development. Certain personal values may be overdeveloped or underdeveloped region by region. This should not preclude an overarching target descriptor of the commonalities.

Look at the values of the customer. What opinions, attitudes, interests, and beliefs differentiate the target customer? Does this target like predictability? How about adventure? Is this a traditionalist or a free spirit? Does the target believe there is too much information available or not enough? Does this person want brands knowing a lot about her or knowing just a little?

The agreed personal values go into the Customer Values level of the Brand Pyramid. Then, with this agreed "person" in mind, the next step is to define the functional, the emotional, and the social benefits that will appeal to this prospect and differentiate our brand. These go into their respective levels of the Brand Pyramid.

The Brand Personality is a succinct definition of the distinctive personality characteristics that will be relevant and motivating to the particular target customer.

Building a Brand Pyramid is a group effort. Once the information is generated, Global Brand Leadership will sort it into the four levels of the Brand Pyramid (functional benefits, emotional and social benefits, customer values, brand personality). In the spirit of shared responsibility, this summary will capture the thinking of all the regions. Although the input of every CFT member is respected, the responsibility for the ownership of the agreed, final Brand Pyramid is global.

Global Brand Leadership manages the process, facilitates the discussion, ensures that everyone participates, respects all input, and leads the synthesis. The input is 50/50, and the output must reflect the input.

2. Brand Promise

A Brand Promise[3] statement summarizes in a brief sentence (or two) the special contract that exists between a brand and its target audience (see Figure 8.5). It succinctly describes what the brand is intended to stand for in the mind of a specific group of customers or prospects. By consistently living up to the Brand Promise, we can ensure that our brands will be relevant and distinctive.

For people with these values...	
Who seek these rewards/social benefits...	
Brand X, with this personality...	
Provides these functional benefits...	
Because it has these features...	

Figure 8.5 Brand Promise statement

The Brand Promise defines the essential relevant differentiation of the brand expressed (see Figure 8.6). Creating the Brand Promise is also based on a shared 50:50 collaboration. It is a creative editing exercise that extracts the selected key words and ideas from each of the levels of the Brand Pyramid. It does not have every word and idea from the Brand Pyramid. The Brand Promise is a succinct, short statement that will define the relevant differentiation of the brand.

For people with these values...	Welcome change
Who seek these rewards/social benefits...	Feel contemporary and cool
Brand X, with this personality...	Knowledgeable, innovation leader
Provides these functional benefits...	Brilliant solutions in the modern world
Because it has these features...	Technology expert, proven record

Figure 8.6 Brand Promise statement—example

Here is a summary template for defining a Brand Promise:

- For people with these values... (Fill in the essential differentiating personal values of the customer/prospect from the Values level of the Brand Pyramid.)

- Who seek these rewards/social benefits... (Fill in the essential differentiating emotional rewards/social benefits of the customer/prospect from the Emotional/Social Benefits levels of the Brand Pyramid.)

- Brand X, with this personality... (Fill in the essential differentiating personality elements of the brand from the Personality level of the Brand Pyramid.)

- Provides these functional benefits... (Fill in the essential differentiating functional benefits of the customer/prospect from the Functional Benefits level of the Brand Pyramid.)

- Because it has these features... (Fill in the key supporting features of the brand from the Features level of the Brand Pyramid.)

3. Brand Lotus Blossom[4]

The Brand Lotus Blossom integrates the Brand Essence with its set of Guiding Principles and the Brand Essence dictionary. The Brand Pyramid and Promise are important. They are the starting point upon which the rest of the process is based. But the Brand Promise is six phrases. To achieve organizational alignment, it is easier for most of the organization to deal with a shorthand way of expressing the Brand Promise. This is the role of the Brand Essence: it is an inspirational, short (two or three words) way to communicate what the brand stands for. Intended for internal audiences and for close partners and suppliers, it is enormously helpful for advertising agencies and other creative partners. It provides the thematic, internal brand phrase that enables consistent communication and integration across the organization.

Not a Slogan

The Brand Essence is not for external use. It is an internal guidepost for all who work on behalf of the brand. The Brand Essence phrase should be something that can unite the organization around the core brand idea. It is not meant to be an advertising slogan. All brand actions should be consistent with and reinforce the Brand Promise and the Brand Essence.

The Guiding Principles

The Guiding Principles help dimensionalize the brand experience. These Principles describe how we want our customers to feel as they experience our brands. For each of the Guiding Principles, we define how each principle supports the Brand Essence. This is the Brand Dictionary definition of each principle.

Why is it necessary to have a common brand language? The same words may have very different meanings to different people around the world. Saying the same thing but not meaning the same thing is dangerous. Internally, we should mean the same things when we say the same things. Consistency is critical.

So, for each Guiding Principle, we find three to five specific defining words. All the language generated becomes the Brand Essence Dictionary. As with any dictionary, this one clearly commits the organization to what we mean by each Guiding Principle. The Brand Essence Dictionary provides a common and consistent language for all branded marketing.

Lotus Blossom

The final output can be displayed as a Lotus Blossom (see Figure 8.7). The Lotus Blossom defines the relevant and distinctive brand experience we want our customers to have. The Brand Essence is at the center and serves as the brand anchor. The petals surrounding the center are the Guiding Principles. Once the Guiding Principles are agreed upon, it is important to define each of them, as you would see in a dictionary. The same words can mean different things to different people; to avoid confusion, it's necessary to create the brand Lotus Blossom. That way we all mean the same thing when we define the brand.

Creation of the Brand Essence, the Guiding Principles, and the defining terms is again a creative task. It is the role of Global Brand Leadership to manage this creative process, facilitate as the whole team discusses each part of the Lotus Blossom, and help achieve final agreement.

The goal is to agree to a two- to three-word Brand Essence and three to six Guiding Principles (petals) surrounding the core essence of the brand. Each principle must have a "dictionary definition" so that everyone defines the Guiding Principles the same way (see Figure 8.8).

Global Brand Leadership finalizes the output after much iteration. However, the Lotus Blossom as well as all the other elements in Box 2 must be reflective of all regional input. Not everyone will agree 100% of the time. Regional leaders have the opportunity to be creative within the Framework in Box 3.

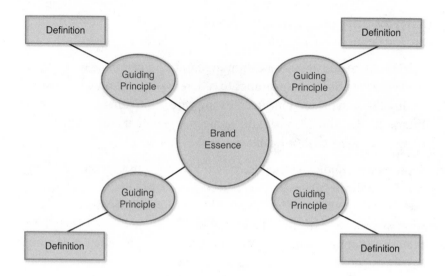

Figure 8.7 Brand Lotus Blossom

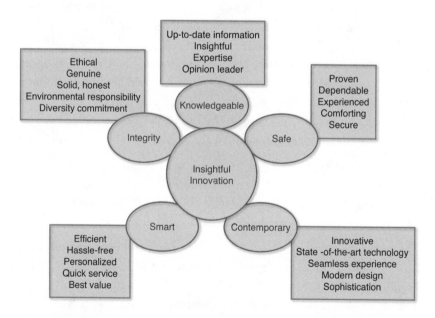

Figure 8.8 Brand Lotus Blossom—example

4. Brand Framework

The Brand Framework describes the nonnegotiable boundaries and policies that define the brand's common, global, total brand experience. The Framework creates the brand's global boundary lines within which the brand is to be communicated and delivered. The Brand Framework is cocreated with regional and functional teams collaborating to define global commonalities while allowing freedom (in Box 3) for respecting local nuances. Like before, this is a 50/50 collaborative document. (We use the word "document" to mean either a written printed document or a written electronic communication.) The Global Brand Leadership leads and guides the discussions and the composition of the Brand Framework. However, once again, the collaborative nature of Box 2 demands that regional leaders have a responsibility to participate and provide direction and insight. Global Brand Leadership must be a very cooperative colleague, not a commandant.

The Brand Framework builds on the Brand Pyramid, Brand Promise, and Lotus Blossom (Brand Essence, Guiding Principles, and Brand Essence Dictionary). It includes the brand vision and the description of the target audience(s). It delineates nonnegotiable items that have to do with people, product, place, price, and promotion, such as the defined product, service and design guidelines, service behaviors, specific brand standards, trademark policy, and pricing policies.

It is everyone's responsibility to activate and evaluate all action on behalf of the brand against this Framework. The Brand Framework is a dynamic document that is improved, deepened, and refreshed over time to reflect new learning and to keep the brand relevant.

Freedom within the Framework

When it comes to local marketing activation, the Brand Framework rests and operates on an important principle: Freedom within the Framework. Freedom within the Framework allows for local and regional relevance within the globally agreed guardrails that ensure global coherence. The Brand Framework is the bridge across the global-regional divide. This principle means that all those working on behalf of the brand are encouraged to be creative within the boundaries of the Framework in determining how to attract customers and potential customers.

Freedom within the Framework is all about regional and local creativity. But creativity will not flourish if we do not create a creative-friendly environment. It cannot just be global that "freely" generates the ideas. Regional and local leaders who are closest to the "point of sale" have ideas as well. Creativity is a two-way street.

Our Model is not just about process. It is also about creating an environmental mind-set that does not stifle creativity but focuses it. It creates an environment where creativity is welcome, where it can flourish, not famish. Brands need ideas to stay fresh and relevant. With the Freedom within the Framework principle, the CFT creates an atmosphere that feeds rather than impedes creativity for the entire branded organization. Freedom within the Framework creates the hospitable environment, the fertile ground for great creativity to happen. A Brand Framework provides the discipline and the boundary lines. Within these boundary lines, there is room for creative freedom: the free-thinking expression, the freedom of thought, and the fertile ground for idea generation.

There will be differences company by company, but for this purpose, here is an example of a Table of Contents for a Brand Framework:

Brand Ambition

Target Audiences, Values, Needs, Problems, Occasions

Brand Promise

Brand Pyramid and Brand Lotus Blossom

> Brand Essence

> Guiding Principles

> Brand Essence Dictionary

Brand Design Principles

Brand Icons

Brand Standards

Brand Policies

> Trademark

> Design

> Communications

Sustainability

Pricing

Retail, Channel, Outlets

Media

Digital

Mobile

Social networking

It takes full collaboration to create a proper Brand Framework. It sets the boundaries for the brand, but it is not a straightjacket. Within the boundaries of the Framework, regional and local leaders and managers have the responsibility to use their creativity, their judgment, their intuition, and their expertise to generate and implement the appropriate actions on behalf of the brand. Just like football/soccer has a boundary, when generating the regional ideas, be creative and use your skill within the boundaries. You cannot take the ball out of bounds.

Freedom can be frightening. Regional and local leaders and managers may complain that they are not given a chance to contribute when they are mere order-takers for global initiatives. With global centralization, local management abdicates accountability for results. However, following Freedom within the Framework, local management must utilize their freedom to take their own actions, follow their own judgments, and take responsibility. The accountability that results from those freedoms is often uncomfortable.

With one client, some regional leaders were uncomfortable when they realized that they were accountable for designing and executing regional and local differentiation within the Framework. They suddenly realized that they did not have the right people in place with the necessary talent; did not have sufficient resources; and, sadly, did not have the stomach for that much responsibility.

In our earlier discussion, we explained the power that localization and regionalization have on a global brand. Freedom within the Framework is a way to liberate regional and local teams by providing the room to design for the cultures, mores, styles, and tastes of a specific region while maintaining the core essence of the global brand. Freedom within the Framework allows for regional and local brand entrepreneurial spirit.

Furthermore, Freedom within the Framework optimizes the return on global learning. It allows the entire branded organization to benefit from the many efforts of various areas of the world while being able to keep the brand true to its core. Global solidarity with national strengths is the best combination.

5. Brand Book

It is essential to create a compilation of the Brand Promise and Guiding Principles in book form. This can be electronic or printed, or both. It should be a brochure that in a short-hand manner illustrates what the brand stands for, why consumers want it, and what the desired brand experience is that you want the consumers to receive. It should capture the look and feel of the brand. Think of this as a brand bible that gives you the necessary information by capturing and describing the core brand story in words, examples, and pictures. A good Brand book should describe the following information:

- The Brand Promise
- The Brand's Guiding Principles and discuss the consumer experience
- The brand's service style
- The brand's target audience and his/her needs and problems
- Current and soon-to-happen solutions for the target's problems

6. Global Brand Plan to Win

The Global Brand Plan to Win[5] defines the brand's global focus, the action implications across the five Action Ps—people, product/service, place, price, and promotion—and the global performance objectives. The Global Brand Plan to Win includes metrics to evaluate whether we are making measurable progress.

The Global Brand Plan to Win follows the eight P structure: purpose, promise, people, product, place, price, promotion, and performance. We define these as follows:

- **Brand Purpose (Ambition)**—The common goal for all the actions on behalf of our brand. It is our brand destination. It defines the True North of the brand. Organizational alignment is critical. The entire organization must be aligned behind a single, clear, shared goal for each of our brands.

- **Brand Promise**—Summarizes the brand's focus. It directs how we will develop the connection between the brand and our customers. Brand Promise summarizes in a brief statement the special contract that exists between a brand and its customers. By consistently living up to a brand's Promise, we can ensure that our brands will be relevant, distinctive, powerful, and great.

- **Five Action Ps**

  - **People**—Employees are the most important asset to any business. They are the frontline when it comes to customer relationships, especially in a service business. Internal brand pride is a critical success factor affecting external brand attitudes. If we want employees to have passion and pride in our delivering a superior brand experience, we have to show them we have passion and pride in what they do and who they are.

  - **Product (and Service)**—The tangible evidence of the truth of the brand promise. A brand needs to be relevantly differentiated, delivering superior customer-perceived value. Continuous renovation and innovation are imperative for success. Product and service renovation and innovation are keys to sustainable profitable growth.

  - **Place**—Refers to any location where the sale is made and can equally include a physical location (a restaurant, for example) as well as a virtual one (a website, for example). Wherever and whatever it is, place is the face of the brand.

  - **Price**—This is an important part of the customer's value equation. It is the denominator of the Trustworthy Brand Value equation. Value is determined by the total branded experience a customer expects (functional, emotional, and social benefits) for the price spent (in terms of time, money, and effort) multiplied by trust.

- **Promotion**—This is about creating an integrated approach to raising awareness, familiarity, and preference of the brand. Promotion includes every communication on behalf of the brand.

- **Performance**—Metrics that will be used to evaluate the progress toward the achievement of the brand purpose and brand promise through implementation of the activities of the five Action Ps.

A Global Brand Plan to Win sets a high bar for the brand. It reflects the vision and forward nature that is necessary for proper, disciplined strategic thinking. It provides planning boundaries and sets up a future focus. A Regional Brand Plan to Win by its very nature must focus on what is happening now in the region. It is more focused on short-term results. A coherent brand needs both kinds of eyesight. The Regional Action Plans must be executed within the context of the Global Brand Plan to Win.

Box 2 presents challenges. It is not easy to ensure that executives will share in a 50/50 manner when it affects their "territories." It is a struggle. But the struggle is worth it because in our changing, integrated world, executives who cannot understand or live with collaboration and sharing will find themselves on the wrong side of enduring profitable growth. Collaboration is time consuming and takes energy. Some people will merely get along to go along and then do their own thing. This attitude is detrimental to growing coherent, global powerful brands.

Making Box 2 Work

1. Ensure Collaboration

Collaboration and coordination are not the same. The One-Box and Two-Box models of global marketing are all about coordination. Coordination is from Latin: *Co* means together and *ordinare* means to order; keeping things in order is the gist of coordination. Coordination is about organizing different elements and activities of a process to enable them to work efficiently. The One-Box and Two-Box models' primary focus is on efficiency. We coordinate activities, calendars, and meetings.

Collaboration is different. It is about people jointly working together to produce or create something to achieve shared goals. It means learning from each other, helping to build and nurture ideas, sharing information, intuition, and initiative. It means working together to make things work better. It is about more than efficiency; it is effectiveness.

Companies need to ditch the dictatorship and give the hand-off approach the heave-ho. With a world in flux, we have the opportunity to transform global marketing from a partitioned responsibility approach to a true collaborative approach to building strong brands.

2. Open the Discussion to Ideas from Everywhere

Avoid the problem of people owning an idea and not giving it room to breathe. One of the key principles underlying The Collaborative Three-Box Model is that good ideas do not care where they come from. Dominant regions should not dominate creativity. It is not the size of the country that counts; it is the size of the idea. Accept ideas even if they come from small countries or people with different perspectives and skills. In many cases, organizations look downward on regions and regional ideas. So brand-building ideas from regions and locales are dismissed. Or ideas are dismissed because they originate from people who are in functions that are not designated as requiring marketing expertise.

This is a marketing sin. Brands cannot afford to leave ideas out of the loop because they are associated with people, places, and functions outside the marketing center or outside the central marketing function.

We agree with the great nineteenth century railroad mogul Cornelius Vanderbilt who said, "You never know where a good idea comes from." He was right. Great ideas do not care where they come from or who has them. Similarly, each geography or function should be open to ideas from others outside their local geography or function.

Great creativity has universal appeal; great ideas can come from anywhere. Global organizations are creative communities with talented resources that are virtual cauldrons of creativity, with worthy ideas swirling around and around the world.

Collaboration fosters idea dissemination. Great ideas do not always come from a single source. Brands need to tap into this huge reservoir of creative talent residing within our regional and local communities. Think of this as reaching into a community chest filled with ideas from all our talented resources. The free flow of the ideas will help to shape the brand, using the collective intelligence and sensitivity of everyone from everywhere.

3. Build a Compliance Process

The Collaborative Three-Box Model must have a forum for raising issues of noncompliance with the Framework. Every organization will treat this differently depending on the culture, roles, and job descriptions. Noncompliance with the program affects the brand as well as the branders. Along with time, energy, and other resources being put into changing the mind-set and the marketing approach, there needs to be a court of higher appeal. People need to know that there will be consequences for noncompliance. There should be penalties for defaulting to business as usual or doing things outside the Framework. We will discuss this in Chapter 9, "The Collaborative Three-Box Model: Box 3—Bring the Brand to Life." Activities outside the Framework need to be stopped, activities inside the Framework need to be supported, and ideas from regions in Box 1 and Box 2 need to be encouraged.

Lessons Learned: Box 2

Lesson One: Focus on Strategy, Not Tactics

Box 2 develops the Global Brand Framework. This is a dynamic, strategic document that does not include tactics. Tactics can wait for the planning at the regional level. Yet, when there is friction and tension between "colleagues," the conversations tend to devolve to the tactical level: "Okay, here is what we want the brand to do." The Global Brand Framework represents the nonnegotiable boundaries within which the regions must take responsibility for creating actions, but that is Box 3. Box 2 is difficult because the leadership is split 50%/50%. So when in doubt, tactical discussions are easier than strategic ones. A client introduced a European line of products into the United States. They focused on selecting an attention-getting celebrity. They did not first define the intended brand character to guide the celebrity decision. This is why the Lotus Blossom must be developed with such attention to "how we want the customer to feel." The new definition of value—Trustworthy Brand Value—has the total branded experience as the numerator: functional, emotional, and social benefits. To increase value, defining these before creating the tactics is the logical approach to success.

Lesson Two: Understand the Difference between the Levels of the Brand Pyramid

Knowing the difference between a functional benefit, an emotional reward, and a social benefit is helpful when conducting market research, for example. Recently, we helped a client create a Brand Promise and Brand Essence for a brand. For functional benefits (what the brand *does*), we were told that the items for the Brand Pyramid should be features like bright lights, clear signage, Wi-Fi, and open 24 hours. The items listed here are features or the tangible support that makes the Brand Promise real for the customer. Features are tangible attributes that make the brand's claim credible. Features are not benefits. Features, like tactics, are easier to think about. Features are more tangible—things you can ascertain by the five senses. But features are not the relevant functional, emotional, or social benefits that will differentiate the brand. When defining the Emotional and Social Rewards level of the Brand Pyramid, there is a tendency to stick with generic feelings, such as "I feel good" or "I feel smart." Filling in the Brand Pyramid is similar to peeling an onion: What are the functional benefits? How does that make the customer feel? Why did you say that? Feeling good is positive, but specifics are important when building a differentiating Brand Promise Statement. With a properly developed Brand Pyramid, a Brand Promise Statement, and a Lotus Blossom, the various functions can do their jobs better. At Nissan in the first phase of the turnaround, Shiro Nakamura, the newly appointed head of Design, posted the Brand Pyramid, Promise, Lotus Blossom, and Essence on the walls of the studio so everyone knew what the intended brand experience was for new Nissan designs.

A word of caution: one of the roles of Global Brand Leadership is to ensure the integrity of the Brand Framework. In one recent instance, a client hired an architectural firm to design some new structural elements for the brand. None of the plans reflected the key criteria of the

Brand Pyramid, Promise, and so on, because the architects felt these "impeded the creativity" of their project team. The newly designed structural elements were fabulous—just not for this particular brand. Work was halted until the plans were brought back inside the Framework. Vigilance is a most valuable asset for Global Brand Leadership.

Lesson Three: The Brand Framework Is a Liberating Document

We once worked with a dynamic, entrepreneurial company that owns some successful brands. One time, the creative leader pointed out that her creativity needs boundaries. She made a little cup with her hand and said that creative people need to know where the cup's sides are. It is more effective to work within a cup than spill over the sides and make a mess of the brand.

The Brand Framework is the cup, a cauldron of creativity. And yes, it has boundaries to protect the core of the brand. One of the most disputed parts of the Framework is the brand's policies. We spoke of pricing policies. We are talking about the policy behind the pricing; we are talking about a monetary policy for building Trustworthy Brand Value. All governments have pricing policies. So, too, should brands. Trademark policy is critical as well, yet it is the policy that is often violated or ignored by branders who believe that trademark policies constrain brand creativity. Most brand and marketing people are woefully ignorant of trademark policy and in some cases behave as if it were something the legal department throws in the way of generating sales.

One global client wanted to expand the brand into new countries only to find out that the brand name was not protected in most of the new and many of the existing countries. Another client spent eight months with a name consultant trying to find a name for a new brand. And then it was only protected in the United States because there were countries where a version of the name was already in use. Also, an established brand in the United States determined that one of the brand's product names referred to a sexual act in a foreign language. Brand marketers sometimes overlook trademark policies and then turn to the legal teams to sort things out.

Everyone is accountable for how the brand is managed and built within the Brand Framework. No one has a free pass. No one can say, "I did not know that."

Endnotes

1. American blues song first recorded by John Lomax in 1934; Asch Recording, writer unknown.

2. See Light, Larry and Kiddon, Joan, *Six Rules for Brand Revitalization: Learn How Companies Like McDonald's Can Re-Energize Their Brands*, Wharton School Publishing, Pearson Education Inc., NJ, 2009, pp. 78–79.

3. Ibid., Light and Kiddon, p. 79.

4. Ibid., Light and Kiddon, pp. 81–83.

5. We devoted a large part of our previous book on the Plan to Win. Please see Light and Kiddon, Chapter 6.

9

The Collaborative Three-Box Model: Box 3—Bring the Brand to Life

I'm free
I'm free
And freedom tastes of reality

—The Who[1]

Localism and personalization are strong forces for change. Box 3 is the opportunity for the cross-functional team (CFT)—with the Regional Leadership and local managers guiding the process—to show how creative they will be within the Framework. It is the regional opportunity to "fly with freedom." The outputs of Box 3 detail the localized actions that will take place within the Brand Framework. Local plans, locally delivered personalization, and accountability for local results are local responsibilities. "Nothing happens until it happens at retail" means that a large part of the brand experience happens at the point of exchange. It means that you order the pizza online and it is made and delivered locally. It means you call the hotel concierge—not the hotel HQ—about your dry cleaning. It means you bring your car in for service at your local dealership; you do not take it to Detroit or Mississippi or Yokohama. It means that you experience the benefits of Tide detergent when you purchase it at your store in your neighborhood and use it your way in your machine in your home with your laundry. To be successful, global leadership needs the input and activation of local teams. Globalization thrives when it is combined with local relevance and personal differentiation.

Box 3 responsibilities are weighted 20% global and 80% regional, the reverse of Box 1. The Freedom within the Framework principle, as discussed in Box 2, must be strictly enforced. It guides all the thoughts and actions on behalf of the brand at the regional level. The Global Brand Leadership provides support, thought leadership, and governance to ensure alignment with all the elements of the Framework.

The Regional Brand Leadership designs and executes the Total Brand Experience to meet the needs of the regional and local customers. Of course, the regionally/locally designed experience must be within the Framework maintaining the brand's global commonalities. The purpose of Box 3 is local relevance and locally delivered personalization; these elements create the branded experience. No one knows how to bring the relevant local situation, opportunities, and challenges to life as well as the regional and local brand teams.

Not a Hand-Off

Box 3 is not a hand-off.

Box 3 is not about Global Brand Leadership handing over the brand to Regional Brand Leadership to then do with it what it wants. Those Regional Brand Leaders who believe that they now have completely free rein are behaving in a noncollaborative and brand-eroding manner. Box 3 is all about working together for the good of the brand *within the Framework*. Regional Brand Leadership must engage the Global Brand Leadership so they can provide support, thought leadership, global knowledge sharing, and branded governance to ensure alignment within the Global Brand Framework.

Decision Rights

The regional teams own the decision rights regarding regional and local actions taken within the Brand Framework. The global teams have veto rights if a regional action is outside the Framework. However, as with any power of the veto, it should rarely be used. The Collaborative Three-Box Model is centered on the idea of collaboration, not confrontation.

As indicated in Figure 9.1, there are four components of Box 3:

1. Local Brand Ambition and SMART Objectives
2. Local Total Brand Experience including in locale, region personalization
3. Local Problems and Drivers
4. Local Brand Plan to Win

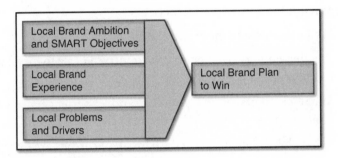

Figure 9.1 Three-Box Model—Box 3

1. Local Brand Ambition and SMART Objectives

This is similar to the last step in Box 1, but it is created to reflect the local differentiated environment including the competitive situation. How will the brand be competitive in this region? What is different about the customer's perceived competitive set? How will the brand drive Trustworthy Brand Value in this region? How different is the "category" in this region? What are the specific local objectives? This is the chance to articulate relevant differences and uniquely personal delivered ideas relative to the global brand ambition.

As we stated while describing Box 1, SMART Objectives describe the measurable goals that must be met to ensure we are on the right track toward achieving the Ambition. The definitions of the SMART Objectives are the same for the local version as for the global version:

- Specific
- Measurable

- Aspirational yet achievable
- Related to overall business growth
- Time specific

2. Local Total Brand Experience

Here are just some of the questions that must be addressed in this part of Box 3:

- What is the Total Brand Experience?
- Is this the same in the entire region?
- Are there differences country to country? Locale to locale within a country?
- What elements of the global brand experience need to be consistent?
- What global elements have the consistent core yet are interpreted appropriately so that the brand is locally relevant?
- In what way is the local Total Brand Experience delivering personalization?

The questions reflect the ongoing debate about a brand's Total Brand Experience: where does responsibility for the Total Brand Experience sit? "Who owns it?" is a frequently debated issue.

In The Collaborative Three-Box Model, the Total Brand Experience may be delivered locally, but that local delivery must be within the boundaries of the Global Brand Framework. Local and personal understanding is the area of expertise of the local brand teams. Ensuring compliance is the role of Global Brand Leadership.

The Total Brand Experience has many stages, sometimes called the customer journey. The customer experience begins before the customer has actually purchased a brand or service. The search experience, the information sorting experience, the website checking of reviews and ratings, and the experience of asking friends and family members—any or all of these may happen before a short list of possible brands is even prepared. Category knowledge adds to the search criteria. Of course, the short list is often based on previous experience or just on brand familiarity and reputation.

From a brand perspective, there will be elements of the customer's experience that must be globally or nationally consistent, customer-to-customer, such as the definition of the core brand promise. There will also be elements on the web page that can be immediately localized and personalized even if it is as small as the callout of your name welcoming you back to the site.

Customization or personalization can happen well before the purchase, changing the brand experience to fit the user and her friends. In today's marketing environment, there is frequent discussion that marketers "own" less and less of the brand experience as customers increasingly co-create the experiences they want to have.

> "As a marketer, you can't build the customer journey anymore. To enable customers to design their own journeys and for marketers to be there to meet customer expectations is to drive long-term value through retention marketing."
>
> —Neil Capel, CEO and founder of Sailthru[2]

Localization within the Framework

This is why there is heated discussion at the Box 3 level when talking about "how the customer experiences the brand," and about "who is in charge of making this a favorable experience." The sharing economy is not just about the collaborative use of goods and services; it is also about improving and evolving brand perceptions. However, constant vigilance is required. The core essence of the brand needs to have consistencies that are understandable worldwide. Total Brand Experience will have common elements and relevant differentiating elements before you even arrive at the personalization for customers.

For example, a Toyota has a series of design cues that make it a Toyota. However, there will also be elements that change geographically. The Framework identifies those brand elements that must remain consistent. These are the global elements that deliver the Toyota-ness. This sense of Toyota will have been agreed upon in the Box 2 section on Brand Framework building. Some of these elements will become brand standards (that is, those elements that are consistent across geography and a must-have for delivering the core brand essence).

McDonald's has core menu items that should be consistent, such as Big Mac and French fries. However, in France, the menu also includes soups, and sandwiches use French cheeses. And now McDonald's is increasing local flexibility to create menu variation within a country, including the United States.

Even within the same area in the same state, different stores may have different items. For example, Whole Foods in Palm Beach Gardens, Florida, does not have the same array of artisan vegan products as the Whole Foods in Boca Raton, Florida, even though these stores are both in the same area in Florida. Why? The fellow behind the cheese counter who knows the SKUs of the artisanal nondairy cheeses says that Boca Raton is the more upscale store with the greater demand; therefore, it receives the shipments of nondairy cheeses first. Artisanal nondairy cheeses are not as popular in Palm Beach Gardens.

In fast-moving consumer goods, the mix of items may vary from local market to local market. In India, Dunkin' recognizes that Indians are not particularly fond of doughnuts. While they still serve doughnuts, they also created new morning foods, such as non-beef burgers that come with spicy vegetables or potatoes.[3]

Haier changes products by country to satisfy regional needs and solve regional problems. In Pakistan, Haier has large washing machines that can handle Pakistani robes; in China the washing machines are either small for the delicate items or ones that have industrial hoses for washing vegetables on farms. The machines are also tailored by locale to eliminate specific pollutants in more than 220,000 different communities.[4]

The Total Brand Experience covers service behaviors. Some are global, and some service behaviors are localized to fit the country and the culture. In China's McDonald's, there are "baby-sitters" who help parents with their children. The training varies. What is defined as "friendliness" is different in different countries.

Personalization within the Framework
We discussed personalization in the beginning of this book. In a "retail" environment, personalized actions happen at the "store" level, such as

a hardware store, a car dealership, a restaurant, a hotel, a bank or an online store such as Amazon. Personalization is having your name, your preferences, and your list pop up when you log on to Drugstore.com.

Tide now runs communications emphasizing "my Tide" and showcases the different ways that customers use the Tide line of products. By showing that different people with different needs can combine Tide's offerings in many ways, Tide is becoming more personal. M&M's allows you to create your own color schemes and initials to make the candy-coated confectionary your very own for your very own occasions. Lay's asks you to "Do Me a Flavor" by suggesting your personal taste choice for a new Lay's potato chip.

A pizza chain has software that recognizes the caller from the telephone number. The software recalls the address of the previous deliveries as well as what was ordered. This makes the whole order experience easier, quicker, and more personal.

Local Manager Is the Ultimate Brand Manager

Local Managers are the ones who make sure that each one of the customers has a great branded experience. This is especially important in the service business. General managers are responsible for ensuring that the brand lives up to its promises and creating the individualized brand experiences. They localize. They personalize.

Think about all the things that a local manager knows and manages:

- The local manager knows the customers best.
- The local manager knows the customer's needs and behaviors.
- The local manager knows the customer's problems and concerns.
- The local manager knows the neighborhood.
- The local manager knows the business community and the potential for building strong local business relationships.
- The local manager is responsible for local area marketing.
- The local manager is in charge of community outreach.

The local managers are the ultimate brand managers. Working with the general managers of a store, a restaurant, a ship, a theater, a hotel, an airline lounge, and so forth, is the first step in creating the relevant, differentiated Total Brand Experience in a local market.

3. Local Problems and Solutions

Because so much customer engagement happens in real time in the actual location—at retail, in a hospital or hotel, on a cruise, in a movie theater, at a café or school, or online—knowing what problems people have with the brand and developing the best solutions and solutions for positive engagement is essential. Domino's Pizza's research indicated that customers had serious concerns with the quality of its pizzas. Customers had problems with the crust, with the sauces, with the toppings, and with the cheeses. It was a barely edible concoction. The Domino's brand differentiator was focused on delivering pizzas fast, so that's what it devoted resources to. But the pizzas the company was delivering were awful. Who cares if a customer can get a pizza delivered quickly if he don't want to eat it when it arrives? So Dominos finally decided to create better tasting pies. It bravely addressed the quality reputation problem head on in marketing communications. Domino's successfully resurrected the brand through problem-solution.

The best way to get started on identifying problems and solutions is to mine current market research. It would be extremely helpful if there were a properly designed problem identification study. A problem identification study uncovers problems with the category, with behaviors in the category, with the brands within the category, and with your particular brand in general. Identifying drivers of satisfaction are also insightful.

It is essential that the CFT examine the problems and solutions by the five action Ps (people, product/service, place, price, and promotion) of the Plan to Win and by each stage of the identified customer journey because this will help with development of the Local Brand Plan to Win. This is not only a task of identification; it is a task of prioritization. A brand cannot focus on every problem and every driver at the same time. It is necessary to prioritize. Looking at the top problems that are barriers to achieving the vision and ambition and looking at the top solutions that need improvement and reinforcement provide a tight set of parameters for action. Check for primary problems and primary solutions.

You need to understand the problems in their context before you go about creating solutions. In one instance, a small appliance company learned that its product should be quieter because noise was a mitigating factor in purchase. In trying to fix the problem, the company made the appliance so quiet that customers wondered whether the appliance was actually effective.

4. *Local Brand Plan to Win*

The Local Brand Plan to Win is identical in structure to the Global Brand Plan to Win except the focus is on regional and local freedom within the Global Brand Framework.

Using all the information from the previous elements of Box 3 along with the information and learning from Boxes 1 and 2, the regional team CFT members and regional managers build the Local Brand Plan. The process is not formulaic. Although the organization shares a common discipline and common thought process, the output won't be common thoughts. We want relevant local creativity within the Framework, not the commonplace. We need collaboration, but we do not want a collective of commonality where we all think and do the same things regardless of geography. The critical idea, however, is to be creative *within* the Framework.

As stated, Regional Brand Leadership has ownership of the decision rights in Box 3. But keep in mind that the global teams have veto rights that may be used if a region's planned activities are to the detriment of global brand performance, *even* if it might be beneficial to the regional brand performance. If there is a question as to which approach will be in the brand's best interests, regional teams are the ones that must prove that their contrary opinion is correct for their country *and* the brand rather than asking for Global Brand Leadership to prove the regional/local position is wrong. This is one of the major areas of responsibility of the regions: to prove why the outside-of-the-Framework actions are correct rather than making it the business of the center to prove why global consistency, standards, and the Framework are correct.

Brand Journalism

Box 3 looks at ways to be free and creative within the Global Brand Framework. Mega-brands like Holiday Inn, Coca-Cola, McDonald's, Google, and Amazon appeal to different people in different situations for different needs. This is a major marketing challenge where simplistic distillation of a brand "positioning" to a single word is limiting. How does a megabrand, especially a megaglobal brand, stay relevant in a multidimensional, multifaceted, multiregional marketing world?

One approach is the Brand Journalism concept that gained notoriety when announced by McDonald's in 2004. We have pointed to Brand Journalism several times in this book, but let's examine the concept in detail here. This concept was part of the 2002–2005 successful turnaround that relaunched the McDonald's brand. Positive momentum was created that lasted nine years.

Since that time, Brand Journalism has evolved. It has been adopted, adapted, and scaled by techno-digital, mobile, 24/7 marketers who saw it as a better way to implement the growing focus on what is now commonly called "content marketing." Brand Journalism is a flexible approach for addressing global, regional, local, and personal issues at the same time.

A Little Background[5]

We unveiled the new concept of Brand Journalism at a conference sponsored by *Advertising Age* in June 2004. This was followed by another speech at an ANA conference in August 2004. McDonald's had just experienced a spectacular turnaround, partly because of the new approach to marketing that we called Brand Journalism. This revised marketing approach focused on consumer segmentation rather than the previous excessive focus on product and price promotion.

In 2002, the McDonald's challenge was how to address the needs of different priority consumer segments with different needs in different situations. Brand Journalism was the way we would address multiple targets with specific messages ensuring that all messages were within the boundaries of a common Brand Framework. This assured McDonald's brand consistency around the world. Yet, at the same time, it provided for local marketing flexibility. Brand Journalism addresses the fact that a brand means different things in different regions to different people in different situations: at home, away from home, morning, afternoon, evening, breakfast, lunch, dinner, snack, late night, weekday, weekend, with kids, on a business trip, on a cruise, at a family gathering, at a university, at a wedding, or working all night.

Brand Journalism is a multidimensional, multifaceted way of creating a brand story. By story, we do not mean a fairytale; we mean the compiled history of the brand and its changes and transitions. Every piece of content, every localization, and every personalization adds to the daily log of the brand. The Brand Journalism approach allows a marketer to tell the many facets of the brand story, yet even with these varying communications, customers never lose sight of what they know about the brand and what the brand means.

> "Underlying Brand Journalism is the idea that a brand is not merely a simple word; it is a complex, multi-dimensional idea that includes differentiating features, functional and emotion benefits as well as a distinctive brand character. In this digital, mobile marketing world, no single communication can possibly relate a standardized brand message to every customer that is relevant at the right time for the right reasons."[6]

Brand journalism emerged only 11 years ago when things were very different. True, there were mobile phones receiving email, and there was rapidly evolving technology. Yet the "electronic life" was primitive relative to today. At the time, the idea of Brand Journalism created quite a controversy. Some of the criticism was vehemently negative. Those who embraced traditional marketing approaches expressed outrage that marketing might be evolving and taking a new tact in connecting with consumers. These hard-liner, tradition-bound *positionistas* refused to see that Brand Journalism was not harmful to brands but hugely helpful. They clung to the old-think concept of one brand, one idea, and one word in the customer's mind regardless of how to address the modern marketing requirements of market segmentation, increased localization, and increased personalization. The *positionistas* still cling to their single-minded view of the brand and seem to be disappointed—and even shocked—that Brand Journalism is as relevant today as it was in 2004.

Modern marketing requires that we adopt an approach that informs and maximizes both individuality and inclusiveness. We referred to this earlier as "The Age of I." People want to both be respected as individuals and feel they are members of a community (or communities) of common interests. The digital marketing world allows consumers to express their individuality and be recognized as individuals. At the same time, they are members of a variety of local and global communities satisfying the basic human need of "belonging."

In this global, local, personal world of individualism and inclusivity, consumers want a continuing flow of personally relevant and engaging content—articles, blog posts, live events, videos, and social media. At the same time, they want the ability to express their individual opinions and share these opinions with others. In this ever-evolving, flexible, digital, split-second, techno-laden, app-overloaded, real-time, location-based, mobile environment, Brand Journalism is even more important as a marketing communications platform.

When it comes to modern communications, a single, standardized, inflexible, repetitive brand message with oversimplified content is suicidal. There is nothing appealing about monotone missives today.

Brand Journalism enables marketers to instantly, constantly, and relevantly address the challenges of the globalized-localized-personalized marketing world. Providing new information that can be surprising and delightful helps cultivate an ongoing interest in the brand.

> "Brand Journalism represents a new type of content creation
> that businesses are clamoring to get a grasp of. Quality content
> that enables a more intimate conversation between brands
> and their target audiences is beginning to prove more effective
> than almost any other online marketing strategy."[7]

Brand Journalism communicates an evolving brand story within the brand's consistent global character. At the same time, it can communicate its local differentiation in each country or county or city, along with its personal relevance by segment or by micro segment. Brand Journalism is a natural tool for winning at the intersection of global, local, and personal.

Brand Journalism gives local and regional teams the power to prioritize their activities and tell relevant brand stories that create genuine consumer engagement. At the same time, Brand Journalism strengthens the global brand through coherent brand messages, building global credibility.

Making Box 3 Work

There are several key dynamics that help to make The Model operational, productive, and successful. We discuss these in the following sections.

1. Trust Regional Brand Leadership to Localize and Personalize Well

It is not unusual to hear people in a global function verbally fret over the loss of control to the Regional Brand Leadership. The Global Brand Leadership role sometimes does not trust that the local and regional marketers will do the right things for the brand. It is as if brains and common sense were delivered only to the center and did not make it into the rest of the world. The whole purpose of having a collaborative approach to marketing brands is to work *together* to come up with the best solutions. The Collaborative Three-Box Model gives everyone the option for speaking up. In fact, voicing one's opinion is a responsibility. The Model builds trust among coworkers because everyone is aware of and involved in the plans and strategies all along.

It is not just the external world where trust is in decline, but also internally. Conflicting and competing organizational silos and the fight between global power versus local management accountability lead to internecine warfare to the detriment of the brand. The Collaborative Three-Box Model requires a foundation of trust among the brand builders regardless of where they sit. When a company veers toward excessive centralization or decentralization, there is always a trust issue underfoot. This is why we recommend this guided decentralization approach. The Collaborative Three-Box Model moves the organization toward trusting each other to do the right thing in the right way to achieve the right results on behalf of the brand.

2. Let the Regions Take Accountability for Delivering the Local Brand Experience

Leadership means helping others do what they think is correct. Make it your mission to be a brand leader.

Development of the Brand Framework ensures that the globally consistent components of the global brand experience are codified in Box 2. The Brand Framework creates the boundary lines that must not be crossed. As long as the brand experience work in Box 3 is within the Framework, the Global Brand Leadership must relinquish the reins. However, this is often a cultural mind-set challenge that needs to be overcome. This is why yearly or biyearly meetings on the brand with the CFT members are so important.

3. Support the Brand Journey at All Its Stages

The brand's experience is a journey that starts from thinking, "I might want one of these." This happens whether a customer is considering buying a car or a chocolate bar. The entire experience from start to finish is evaluated on whether it meets expectations. If satisfaction is high, there is a virtuous loop that builds brand preference and loyalty, leading to repeat behavior that is based on true commitment to the brand.

Lessons Learned: Box 3

Lesson One: Manage the Hand-Off Mentality

The Regional Brand Leadership may see Box 3 as their chance to set the record straight when it comes to doing what is right for the brand. From our experience, there is a tendency for Regional Brand Leadership to say, "Thank you very much, Global, but now get out of our way. We will do whatever we think is best in our countries." Then Regional Brand Leadership and teams discard the work of Boxes 1 and 2 and create their own versions of practically everything, including market segmentation and Brand Pyramid, Promise, Lotus Blossom, and Essence. Aside from confusion, this creates hostilities, makes brand-building unproductive, and wastes precious resources. Of course, the brand needs some of its own localization and personalization. The brand also needs to stay relevant and unique to various cultures, temperatures, societies, tastes, values, and so forth. But the core brand must stay intact for it to remain a globally cohesive entity with a core essence transcending and navigating the globe.

The hand-off mentality is harmful to the brand, and thus to the organization as a whole. A brand cannot endure this behavior by the people who should know better: those closest to the customer. This is why there is the Global Brand Framework as a nonnegotiable document. And this is why the Global Brand Leadership has the responsibility to "police" any transgressions outside the Framework.

Imagine that you own a confectionary brand that is based on nougat. Nougat is the single defining ingredient delivering a unique taste, chewiness, and mouth feel. The Pyramid, Promise, Lotus Blossom, and Essence all reflect the special benefits (functional and emotional) of this extraordinary nougat-based product. One day you learn that a certain country's team is changing the nougat to apple butter. Why? A specific country team believes that apple butter is a more distinctive product than nougat. In another instance, the global center learns that a particular regional team does not like the agreed global market segmentation study. The regional team decides to define its own segments and its own product designs. Now, there are two competitive views of the world within the same organization. Even in a relay race, when the baton is handed off to the next runner, everyone is still playing on the same team. Not in marketing with the hand-off mentality. The Collaborative Three-Box Model demands debate and discussion but eliminates, hopefully, the corrosive competitiveness that regional teams set up while defending their positions and the "hey you, get off of my stage" mind-set.

Lesson Two: Meet the SMART Objectives

In creating the SMART Objectives, it is not enough to know what we hope to do; we must know how we are doing locally. We need metrics to evaluate progress. The "M" in SMART stands for "measurable." Are we building brand preference? What is working? Why? What is not working? Why? What are the must-dos and the must-stop actions? It is essential to have the right activities based on the right strategies executed in the right way creating the right results.

At the heart of SMART Objectives is the discussion about the efficiency and effectiveness of the activities. Evaluating progress locally should look at both preactivity and postactivity and then figure out whether this is an activity that should be on the "stop-do now" lists. Regional and global teams dislike "stopping" actions. It is always easier to add than to subtract actions from a plan. At McDonald's, for example, COO Charlie Bell had a rule that if an item was added to the menu board, at least one other item had to come off. Too much confusion stymied customer decision-making and increased the time one waited in line. It is the same for activities. Things were always added but rarely subtracted. The same goes for the brand action plans. A long list of activities makes people look busy, but the result is insufficient resources focused on those things that will really make a difference.

Endnotes

1. The Who, "I'm Free," *Tommy*, 1970.

2. www.sailthru.com, "The Rise of the Individual," Special Advertising Section on Email Marketing, *ADWEEK*, October, 27, 2014, p. E7.

3. Rana, Preetika, "In India, Forget Doughnuts, It's Time to Make the Tough Guy Chicken Burger," *Wall Street Journal*, November 29–30, 2014.

4. Kleiner, Art, "The Thought Leader Interview: Zhang Ruimin, *Strategy & Business*, Issue 77, Winter 2014, pp. 96–102.

5. For a complete discussion on Brand Journalism see Light, Larry, "Brand Journalism: How to Successfully Engage with Consumers in Age of Inclusive Individuality," *Journal of Brand Strategy*, Henry Stewart Publications, Summer 2014, Vol. 3, No. 2. And Light, Larry, "Brand Journalism Is a Modern Marketing Imperative, *Advertising Age*, July 21, 2014.

6. Light, Larry, "Brand Journalism: How to Successfully Engage with Consumers in Age of Inclusive Individuality," *Journal of Brand Strategy*, Henry Stewart Publications, Summer 2014, Vol. 3, No. 2.

7. Business2Community.Com, "Brand Journalism: Cisco's Innovative Approach to Online Content Marketing, September 20, 2012.

PART III

Refreshing the Enterprise

10

Building a Brand Business Scorecard

Numbers don't lie
Check the scoreboard

—Jay Z[1]

Building a Brand Business Scorecard is an essential part of a disciplined brand management process. It is a single integrated report card with metrics that represent business strengths and weaknesses as well as brand strengths and weaknesses. Measuring progress is an imperative component in a meaningful, actionable Brand Plan to Win. This point cannot be stressed enough: meeting measurable milestones is not an option. You need to know where you are headed and if you are making meaningful progress in getting there.

The Brand Business Scorecard has three key business performance measures and eight key brand performance components (see Figure 10.1). The brand performance measures are

Bigger
    Familiarity
    Penetration
Better
    Brand Reputation
    Overall Satisfaction

Stronger
    Brand Preference Ladder
    Trustworthy Brand Value
Trust
    Brand Power

Bigger	Volume, Revenues	Familiarity, Penetration
Better	Market Share	Brand Reputation, Satisfaction
Stronger	Profitability	Brand Preference, Trustworthy Brand Value, Trust, Brand Power

Figure 10.1 Brand Business Scorecard

Bigger

This part of the Brand Business Scorecard tracks the key metrics of brand growth in terms of familiarity and penetration; that is, how well are we known for something special, and how are we doing building the customer base.

Familiarity

Familiarity is not the same as awareness. Awareness is a yes or no question. Are you aware? "Sure, I have heard of him, but I don't have any opinion about him." This is mere awareness. Unfortunately, many researchers and marketers use awareness and familiarity interchangeably. This is wrong. Asking for opinions among respondents who are aware but not familiar provides unreliable, unproductive answers that are a waste of time, money, and effort. Familiarity is more than mere awareness. Familiarity is not an absolute measure; it is measured in degrees, from extremely familiar to not at all familiar.

Penetration

It is always important to gain new customers. Penetration means growing the customer base, with the marketing goal to increase both penetration and loyalty. Attraction and retention are important and are one of the bottom-line goals of the Plan to Win. Attracting customers to a brand is an ongoing, everyday marketing goal. Building loyalty within a declining customer base is just slowing the rate of brand death.

Better

The brand goal is to be better, not just bigger. We need to show improvements in how our brand is perceived. Are we perceived for the things we wish to be perceived for? Are our customers satisfied?

Brand Reputation

Are we delivering on the Brand Promise? Are we delivering against the elements that we agree define our brand? Volvo used to promise to deliver safety. At its best time, this was a differentiating claim. Suburban moms in the 1970s and 1980s drove Volvo wagons. However, Volvo recognized that a brand is more than standing for a single word, so it evolved its brand identity. A relevant, differentiated brand is a multidimensional promise. You can see the elements of the Brand Pyramid in Volvo's evolved description of the new Volvo XC90: "The newest Volvo XC90 captures the essence of the Volvo brand promising a combination of 'bold harmonious design, pure uncluttered luxury, advanced safety and comfort.'"[2]

Pizza Hut is changing to be more like Chipotle in terms of offering a variety of tastes that customers design for themselves. Many marketing and brand commentators have oversimplified the Chipotle differentiation to the single idea of customization. Pizza Hut, McDonald's, and others are trying to copy this attribute thinking that it is how to compete with Chipotle. The Chipotle brand is much more than just customization. At the core of the brand is Steve Ells's passion for providing gourmet quality: "Food with Integrity." Chipotle brand integrity means concern for the welfare of people, animals, and the environment. According to the Chipotle website, "food with integrity is our commitment to finding the very best ingredients, raised with respect for the animals, the environment and the farmers." Chipotle is not sacrificing speed of service while providing customizable food with integrity. As Steve Ells points out, "The problem with fast food isn't that it's fast. It's the food." (www.bonappetit.com, September 16, 2010)

As you can see from these examples, it is essential to truly understand the relevant differentiation of the brand and include specifically designed metrics to reflect these dimensions. To generate the Brand Promise metric, the relevant attributes need to be customized and avoid generic items such as "tastes good," "good value for money," or "convenient."

Overall Satisfaction

This is a topical subject in marketing because brands and organizations rely on overall satisfaction scores for many things, including executive bonuses and employee performance reviews.

Satisfaction is good to have, but it is no longer sufficient. Before JD Power, for example, the automotive industry was uneven in its quality per vehicle. Quality differentiation was easier to communicate. But as quality rose among all the brands, quality differentiation became less observable by new car owners. In the 1990s, there was little meaningful differentiation on overall quality between many automotive brands.[3]

When it comes to customer satisfaction, the competitive bar is being raised. Yet many marketers are aiming for acceptable satisfaction levels. They aim for good enough rather than aiming for "perfection." We recognize that perfection may never be achieved, but why aim for anything less? However, some clients are pleased with 80% satisfaction and very pleased with 90% customer satisfaction ratings. This means they are comfortable with the fact that 10%–20% of their customers are disappointed!

Satisfaction is relative. By relative satisfaction, we mean satisfaction compared to competition. Measure satisfaction not just among a brand's customers but also among the customers of competitive brands. And raise the bar, aiming for the highest levels of satisfaction on whatever metric is being used. Average scores lead to average performance. Average is for losers; excellence is for winners.

Stronger

Building brand strength builds brand value and helps brands withstand competitive pressures.

Brand Preference Ladder

The context for a Brand Preference Ladder is the target audience for the brand. A preference ladder is a staircase leading from nonusage to true brand loyalty; it is a reflection of the strength of the commitment the customer has to the brand relative to competitive brands. Moving customers up the ladder from commodity consideration to true brand loyalty can have a big impact on revenues and profitability (see Figure 10.2).

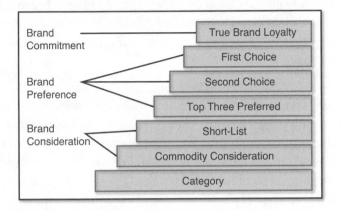

Figure 10.2 Brand Preference Ladder

Commodity consideration means that customers view a set of brands as being basically the same. The customer is actually indifferent and is willing to consider any of these brands. So the differentiator is often merely convenience and price. "Willing to consider" is not the same as, "I would put this brand on my shortlist of brands that I prefer." Being willing to consider is one thing, but moving to being on the short list is a definite competitive advantage.

Shortlist brands are defined as the small set of brands that are among the customer's top three choices. Being on the shortlist is good but not good enough to be a truly strong brand. It is better to be the preferred alternative within the shortlist.

Preference means that of the three brands on the shortlist, this brand (hopefully *your* brand) is the one that a customer prefers. In other words, this is the favorite. Preference is a much stronger concept than satisfaction. For example, customers can be very satisfied with a particular brand of detergent. However, they may also be very satisfied with two or three alternative brands. So they buy the brand that is on sale that week. Satisfaction is necessary, but it is not sufficient. We need to build preferred brands.

The ultimate goal is to move a customer from preference to true brand loyalty. Loyalty is not the same as frequency. Too many so-called loyalty programs build frequency but do not really build loyalty. They build frequency through bribes. They build deal loyalty rather than real loyalty. True brand loyalty is based on a customer's commitment that this brand is the best value.

True brand loyalty is the highest level of commitment on the Brand Preference Ladder. Brands in this category are preferred even though there may be a price premium when purchasing. So imagine that a customer's second choice is 10% less than the preferred, favorite brand. In our metric, a loyal customer would still choose the preferred brand even though her second choice is 10% less. The ultimate brand goal is to increase the number of people who express true brand loyalty.

Trustworthy Brand Value

Marketers often talk about value as low price. That's unfortunate because value is much more than a price point. Brand value decisions need to be strategic. What is the customer-perceived "fair value" for our brand? How are our marketing efforts affecting customer-perceived value? Is price sensitivity increasing or decreasing?

The world does not stand still. A brand may be offered at the same price that worked in the past. But today, that same price is too high compared to competition. Your brand can no longer sustain a price that was considered fair and reasonable in the past. Why? Is it the marketing? Is it changes in quality perception? Is it evolution of the competitive environment? In this increasingly competitive world, excessive emphasis on price incentives may have severely damaged brand loyalty and brand value. Or the brand may have stood still while alternative brands have improved and evolved, raising customer expectations. As we said in Chapter 4, "New Definition of Brand Value," and throughout this book, building Trustworthy Brand Value is essential for enduring profitable growth.

Trust

We devote a lot of time to trust because it is a big issue in marketing today. Trust is a multidimensional idea that underpins and drives relationships. It is an increasingly crucial element crossing many intersections with customers. Do people trust your brand and see it as a trusted information resource? Do they trust what your brand claims and trust that you are doing the right things in the right way? Do they trust what you say about social responsibility? What effect is trust having on your brand's Trustworthy Brand Value equation?

Trust is not a single question. Multiple research studies on trust over the decades show that trust cannot be determined by simply asking, "Is this a trustworthy brand?" Although each research study includes different items in the trust battery, the key word is "attributes" of trustworthiness. Before embarking on the inclusion of a trust "attribute" in a research battery, it is best to include multiple ways to approach trust and to determine trust.[4]

It is also important to determine the drivers of trust for your brand. What is raising or lowering the trust multiplier in your brand's new value equation? What should you stop doing? Start doing? Reinforce? Companies spend a lot of time on drivers of satisfaction and not enough time on drivers of trust. How many times have you taken your car in for a service? Did you have a satisfactory experience? The answer may be "yes." Did that recent satisfactory experience make you trust the brand more than you did before? If this is the fourth time this year that the car needed service, even though you were satisfied this time, the answer is probably "no."

Brand Power

There are many definitions of what makes a powerful brand. But all these tend to view similar components as essential for building brand power. We look at Brand Power in terms of three dimensions: familiarity, specialness, and authority.

As discussed earlier, familiarity is not the same as mere awareness. Familiarity means that the customer is not only aware of the brand but feels he is sufficiently familiar with the brand to express an opinion about it.

Specialness means the combination of both relevance and differentiation.

Authority is the combination of perceptions of overall quality, leadership, and trustworthiness. Quality is driven by a perception of consistent conformance to expectations. Leadership is driven by an image of not only leading in size, but also leading in thought, popularity, and innovativeness. Trustworthy is based on a reputation for credibility, integrity, and responsibility.

Brand Power should be evaluated against the competitive set as perceived by the customer. It is nice to know how your brand rates. But when it comes to making money and satisfying customers, it is necessary to win within the brand's competitive set.

The competitive set is a bigger issue than you might think. We once spoke with a retail client who took us outside of his store as he said, "My competitive set is all the brands I can shop if I turn in a 360-degree circle." All he thought about was that, "If they buy from another store, they have less money to buy from me." Of course, most of the stores in that "circle" were not what *actual customers* thought were his competitors.

Another client in the food industry defined his share goal as "share of stomach." "The more they eat of something else, the less they will eat from my brand." These arbitrary overgrand definitions are not customer defined. This is not how customers make decisions. The customer is the one who decides the competitive set. Within sight of a particular jewelry store in one part of the mall may be a candy store, a maternity clothing store, a hardware store, a sports memorabilia store, a video game store, and a food court. These are not in the customer's competitive set considering the jewelry store.

Building Brand Power can have a powerful effect on brand value. For a UK marketer in durable goods, we determined that a 10% increase in Brand Power led to an incremental £37 per unit. Building Brand Power pays.

A viable Brand Business Scorecard must reflect both business results and brand results. In addition to establishing the metrics, aligning an organization around these common metrics is easier to say than to do. It takes a lot of persistence and fortitude.

Building a proper Brand Business Scorecard needs to be a balance between both business performance and brand performance. The results of the Scorecard should influence the recognition and the reward of the leadership.

Additional Considerations

Here are some additional considerations that must be understood and addressed in order to create the best Brand Business Scorecard.

Five Action Ps

The metrics in the Plan to Win should also include a few specific metrics associated with evaluating the effectiveness of the five Action Ps. We elaborated on the McDonald's metrics in our *Six Rules* book.[5]

There will need to be specific measures for 1) people, such as friendly, helpful, well informed; for 2) product or service, such as quality, speed of service, and accuracy; for 3) place, such as clean, convenient, modern; for 4) price, such as fair value, affordable, range of prices; and for 5) promotion, such as brand familiarity, brand promise, and brand trust. Measures like these allow us to assess progress on the actions we are taking to move our brand forward. The actual measures need to be customized to reflect the specifics of the five Action Ps.

Say Goodbye to Norm

It is in everyone's best interest to ensure that the concept of guided decentralization enhances the move toward common metrics. Of course, no geography wants to give up its traditional measures. All regions have favorites. They have experience with their metrics and they have "Norms"—the normative data collected over the years. However, in a world that spins quickly, "Norm" is losing a foothold. "Norm" no longer defines success.

By embracing "Norm," a brand team is striving to be merely average or somewhat better than average. This is not the same as aiming to be the best or aiming for perfection. The standard is not defined by norms; it is defined relative to competition and relative to the vision of perfection.

Are we doing better than our brand's key competition, and are we making progress toward our agreed destination?

Endnotes

1. Godbey, Chris, Carter, Shawn, Mosley, Garland, Mosley, Timothy, Harmon, Jerome and Cuastellon, Marcos, "Tom Ford," Magna Carta Holy Grail, 2013.

2. www.volvocars.com

3. In the early 1990s, we worked with JD Power data and were able to show exactly this fascinating outcome: as satisfaction increased, differentiation among car brands decreased.

4. There are so many studies to cite on the different ways of approaching trust. Here is a sample of articles that may be of interest. Please note this is a small sample of trust-focused articles. Delgado-Ballester, Elena and Munuera-Alemán, José Luis, "Brand Trust in the Context of Consumer Loyalty," *European Journal of Marketing*, Vol. 35, 11/12, 2001, pp. 1238–1258; Morgan, Robert M., and Hunt, Shelby D., "The Commitment-Trust Theory of Relationship Marketing," *Journal of Marketing*, Vol. 58, No. 3, July 1994, pp. 20–38; Doney, Patricia M., and Cannon, Joseph P., "An Examination of the Nature of Trust in Buyer-Seller Relationships," *Journal of Marketing*, Vol. 61, No. 2, April 1997, pp. 35–51.

5. See p. 152 in Light and Kiddon, *Six Rules for Brand Revitalization*.

11

How Does It All Come Together in an Effective Plan to Win?

Yes, there are two paths you can go by

But in the long run there's still time to change the road you're on

—Led Zeppelin[1]

There is a pathway to global brand success. The common Ambition, Plan to Win, Brand Framework, Freedom within the Framework, and Brand Business Scorecard are the critical elements that bring The Collaborative Three-Box Model to life. They are the ingredients that help ensure there will be global brand coherence with local relevance. This marketing approach is designed to make certain the Ambition and Plans lead to actions producing measurable results. The process requires the discipline to ensure that the global teams will not dominate the thinking or put straightjackets on the creative initiatives of the local teams.

At the same time, the local teams must not ignore the work in Boxes 1 and 2 with the view, "I am responsible for results in my region. So let me do what I think we need to do there." The key is proper and shared allocation of accountabilities, not mere coordination of activities.

As The Collaborative Three-Box Model comes together, there are a few challenges to keep in mind.

Build Real Loyalty, Not Deal Loyalty

Real loyalty is so important that we want to stress again what happens when the brand adopts tactical deals as the priority. Overreliance on deals, discounts, and limited-time price offers is brand destructive. On November 18, 2014, during a U.S. TV segment of "On The Move" (*Bloomberg News*), the commentator Jonathan Ferro spoke of the increase in car registrations in Europe. The numbers were rather remarkable. However, he revealed that incentives per vehicle were running at about 13% discount rate! Thirteen percent off the sticker price is an incredible deal. It is cheaper to buy this new car with its new gadgetry and fuel efficiency than to keep the current "clunker."[2] Mr. Ferro's commentary illustrated that price, not brand, was the important purchase driver. Brands that continue to emphasize price over the brand promise will price-promote themselves into the vicious vortex of operating at the lowest common denominator. This educates the customer to focus just on price alone instead of on brand value. This never-ending, addictive netherworld of deal marketing is death-wish marketing for brands.

Deals do drive purchase and repurchase. But it is a mistake to think that repeated purchases based on deal loyalty are the same as true brand loyalty. Generating revenues based on deals alone is a dark hole from which it is hard to extract a brand. Excessive emphasis on price and incentives creates deal loyalty. Deal loyalty demolishes trusted brands by eroding Trustworthy Brand Value. Real loyalty-building strategies focus on the entire definition of customer-perceived brand value. The Brand Plan to Win articulates the "must-do" actions for building true loyalty to the brand rather than the spurious loyalty that relies only on repeat behavior generated by deals alone.

Consider Both the Long Term and the Short Term

In some organizations, brand building takes a back seat to immediate revenue-generating actions that will produce short-term results. Taking care of the short term is important; if you don't, there will be no long term. However, short-term actions must be executed within the boundaries of the Brand Framework and the directions defined by the Plan to Win. Proper brand actions address both short-term and long-term challenges. Short-termers focus only on results *in* the year, *for* the year. They say they will worry about next year, next year. Every year is a short-term year, and next year never arrives.

This short-term over long-term focus affects innovation. Thinking about the short term means that we will wait to fund innovation next year. When next year arrives, there is no innovation. By the time innovation becomes funded, the competition has moved way ahead. Using short-termism to avoid funding renovation and innovation puts a brand at a major disadvantage, from which it could take years to come back.

In 2014, the *Financial Times* reported that investors are losing their love for companies that focus on the short-term solution to stock price manipulation through share buybacks. Canny investors are buying into companies that are investing in the future—CAPEX. The article refers specifically to a hedge fund manager "who is buying into companies that are undervalued because they are spending heavily now on CAPEX that will generate future returns not yet factored in by the market."[3]

Make the Brand Plan to Win a Force for Alignment

The eight Ps of the Plan to Win reflect both the future and the current actions to generate short-term results and make progress toward our clearly defined brand Ambition. It is an aligning document that creates a road map for global and regional teams to follow. The Plan to Win creates this present and future alignment through the integration of brand actions across the eight Ps:

- Where we want to be: Purpose, Promise
- How we plan to get there: People, Product (Service), Place, Price, Promotion
- How we measure progress: Performance

These eight Ps define a brand-building path to successful, enduring, profitable growth: clearly define where you want to be; focus on the priority actions that will produce both short-term results and build the brand in the agreed direction; and make measurable progress toward where you want to be. A well-crafted Collaborative Three-Box approach keeps everyone on the same page and on track.

In *Six Rules for Brand Revitalization*, we state that Realizing Global Alignment centers on building a Plan to Win.[4] We provide several reasons why this is true. These are worth repeating here with some "updates":

- A Plan to Win is a common platform for rebuilding brand value that is now based on the customer's new value equation: Trustworthy Brand Value. It provides the necessary list of priorities for success. A Plan to Win is also a platform for brand renewal.

- A Plan to Win outlines the critical brand components from Purpose and Promise through the five Action Ps to the measurement of Progress. Inconsistent business and brand building creates global chaos. Our world's volatility and fast-paced change create commotion and confusion. The collision of globalization, localization, and personalization are changing the way a brand becomes powerful. The key trends need to be addressed in those specific ways that make the most sense for the brand. People should have the freedom to do what is best regionally/locally with the Global Brand Framework.

- A Plan to Win creates a common clarity encouraging everyone to aim in the same direction by having the same brand goals and priorities. This clarity refers also to roles and responsibilities. What are the priorities? What are the priority actions? Who is accountable for what actions? A brand cannot become successful or powerful if it is unfocused. Focus is fundamental. It is very noisy around us today, and the Brand Plan to Win clarifies the focal point for the thoughts and arrangements that allow for concentrated activities.

- A Plan to Win helps an organization act as an integrated global/regional cross-functional team (CFT), breaking down functional and geographic silos. Isolation is obstructive and destructive. And it stifles creativity by limiting return on global learning. In a sharing economy, silos are selfish.

Remember: with The Collaborative Three-Box Model, it is necessary to create both a Global Brand Plan to Win and a Regional/Local Brand Plan to Win. The Global Brand Plan to Win looks at the Brand Framework and the Global Brand SMART Objectives, translating these into must-do's. It includes the Brand Ambition, Promise, and Global Performance metrics.

The Regional/Local Brand Plan to Win works within the overarching Brand Framework but reflects the regional and local must-do's, the local SMART Objectives, and the regional or local goals for the global metrics and any key regional or local metrics.

Measure Performance

The Performance P ties it all together. After all, it is all about producing positive outcomes. Developing and adopting common performance measures can be an organizational challenge, especially if there are different existing measures in place in different regions. Each region or country may have its own version of a question for awareness consideration, preference, quality, brand image, overall satisfaction, trust, loyalty, purchase intent, and so on. Although it is common sense that the same metrics should be adopted everywhere, each country will have strong opinions insisting that the other countries use its measures. Each country will have its own favorites. Bringing consistency to this situation of "dueling metrics" takes diplomacy and persistence. After open global discussions, the responsibility for consistency in the metrics is a leadership responsibility. The key is to ensure that both brand and corporate goals are consistently measured, globally and regionally.

Evaluate the Five Actions Ps

Diagnostic metrics must be linked to the five Action Ps in both the global and the regional Plans to Win. For each of the five Action Ps, there need to be a few specific associated metrics; up to three metrics is sufficient. We elaborated on the McDonald's metrics in our *Six Rules* book.[5] There will need to be specific measures for 1) people, such as friendly, helpful, well informed; for 2) product or service, such as quality, speed of service, accuracy; for 3) place, such as clean, convenient, modern; for 4) price, such as fair value, affordable, range of prices; and for 5) promotion, such as brand familiarity, brand promise, and brand trust. Measures like these allow us to assess progress on the actions we are taking to move our brand forward. The actual measures need to be customized to reflect he specifics of the five Action Ps.

A well-crafted Plan to Win is an imperative for any brand, whether global or local. It is most certainly an imperative for a collaborative organization in the modern world. It is a customer-centric document helping to create a customer-centric culture. The promise is all about what the brand will do for the customer and how the customer will feel about the brand. The five Action Ps define the must-do's that will influence the customer's perception of the brand experience. Adherence to the Brand Plan to Win by its very nature will ensure an organization will be a customer-centric culture.

The Collaborative Three-Box Model generates a platform for customer-centricity as well. All the hoarding of data, the pains of relinquishing control, and the fears of new accountabilities are minor compared to the loss of customers because of bickering brand managers and functional leaders. The Model replaces the colleague-contentiousness with customer-centricity. The only consistent source of cash flow is "a customer exchanging money for the brand offer." To take care of the cash flow, we have to take care of the customer. The bottom-line objective is to have more customers, who come more often, are more brand loyal, and who are generating more revenues and more profit. It all begins with a customer focus.

The bottom line of the Plan to Win is more than a blueprint of activities. It is a present-day and long-term document that ensures that everyone involved with the brand at any level and in any function in any geography knows the right things to do in the right way to achieve the right results.

For the brand as well as the organization, trust plays an increasingly central role. Trust is about doing what you say you will do. Trust builds when brands and organizations focus on doing the right things in the right way achieving the right results.

Endnotes

1. Page, Jimmy, and Plant, Robert, "Stairway to Heaven," *Led Zeppelin IV*, 1971.

2. Ferro, Jonathan, "On the Move," *Bloomberg News Television*, November 18, 2014.

3. Foley, Stephen, "Investors No Longer Dazzled by Buybacks Shift Focus to CAPEX," *Financial Times*, November 18, 2014.

4. See Light and Kiddon, Chapter 9, pp. 189–199.

5. See p. 152 in Light and Kiddon, *Six Rules for Brand Revitalization*.

12

Breaking the Bad Habits That
Inhibit Brand Building

History repeats itself because no one was listening the first time.

—Anonymous

It's gonna take time
It's gonna take a whole lot of precious time
It's gonna take patience and time
To do it, to do it, to do it, to do it right

—George Harrison[1]

All the principles and approaches and organizational reconfigurations will not work if companies reinforce habits that stymie growth and innovation. Over the years, we have worked with brands in practically every industry. It is fascinating to see that, regardless of industry, organizations have bad habits that are so pervasive they get in the way of brand-building and culture change. We are not experts in organizational change. But we become part of the organization and observe how these tendencies hamper it.

It is great to have lists of things to do; it is also helpful to have lists of things to avoid. Think of this list of bad habits as a "stop doing it now" list. Bad habits waste money, time, and effort. Everyone always wants to know what to do and that is good; but knowing what to avoid and stop doing is good also. We mentioned some of these throughout this book. Here are some common practices and mind-sets that need to be addressed if The Collaborative Three-Box Model is going to work.

Complacency

For that brief period of time when Charlie Bell was president and then CEO of McDonald's, he would tell us that the one thing that frightened him the most about McDonald's was its ability to slip into the comfort of complacency. Complacency reflects a desire to remain within the comfortable coverlet of the status quo. Once something works, stay with it even if this means never making a change. Doing things the same old way—believing that what worked at one time will continue to work—is turning your back on staying relevant. Complacency is letting things stay the same while the rest of the world is moving ahead; it is uninspiring. It does not instill a passion for the brand; rather, it increases brand passivity. Complacency is a malaise: it is palpable. And it creates a dispiriting depression and desperation. For a while, the effects of positive momentum can cover up the disease of complacency. However, failing to improve, to change, to innovate in a dynamic evolving world is dangerous. Stand still, and the marketing world will pass you by. Just do more of the same in the same way, and you will be punished for your steadfastness.

Change for the Sake of Change

The flip side of status quo is adoption of every idea that is presented. "We need to change" sometimes leads to change for the sake of change. "Every idea is a good idea" is not true. Some ideas are good, but not for this brand. Other ideas are just bad. The challenge is to select the ideas within the Brand Framework that will have the biggest positive brand impact.

Avoid a frenzy of change. Too much change leaves people exhausted, causes enormous confusion, and hurts quality. Several times we have worked with clients who say this is their fourth, fifth, or even sixth president of the division in five years. Each leader feels a need to change everything. Sometimes the pendulum swings from centralization to decentralization and back again in the space of three years. A new CMO arrives, and there is a new advertising campaign or even a new agency. Excessive change results in a cultural attitude that "this too will pass." There is no commitment to the new direction.

Changes do need to happen, but there need to be valid reasons for making changes. These need to be communicated. The organization needs to be inspired, not just informed. People need to be educated as to why the changes are important, what is expected of them, how progress will be evaluated, and so on. Above all, they need to understand and believe that the changes will endure.

Financial Engineering as a Growth Strategy

Financial engineering is a brand killer. It is profitable, but it is not the basis for enduring profitable growth. A primary focus on financial engineering considers the financial community as first, not the customer. Sears, the venerable U.S. retailer, is a good example of this. Sears was hemorrhaging cash at a rate of more than $1.5 billion in 2014. Steven Davidoff Solomon, a law professor at UC Berkeley, wrote a pointed article for the *New York Times* about how the investors in Sears will be paying a steep price for the financial engineering of its owner. He stated that the owner of Sears, "...seems adept at slicing and dicing Sears, but he has failed miserably at turning this business around. He leaves a mystery of how value will be created." Professor Solomon says, "Investors seem to prefer financial tricks at Sears over real results...."[2]

Cost-Managing the Way to Profitable Growth

Just as financial engineering is harmful to brands because it rewards the investor and the analysts rather than the customer, cost management is detrimental to brands. CEOs fall in love with cost management over brand management, but this does not create real sustainable value. You cannot cost-manage your way to enduring profitable growth. Troubled brands receive fewer dollars and other resources. Instead of investing for revitalization and profitable growth, the approach is cutting costs, choking off any possibility of success. These brands are milked, thinned, and then discarded. The result is the unfortunate condition of "*Anorexia Industriosa.*"

Focusing on Customers You Do Not Have at the Expense of Customers You Do Have

It is, of course, important to have both current customers and new customers. However, there does tend to be an attitude that implies, "We already have these customers; let's focus on the customers we do not have." Do not take current customers for granted. There are lots of competitive brands around, and unless you have people who are captive audiences (airlines with specific routes), you run the risk of alienating people who are profitable loyalists. The cable TV companies thought they had the market cornered until satellite dishes became available and affordable. Cable companies thought they weathered the dish onslaught until faced with disrupters such as Netflix and Google TV. AOL behaved in the same way until it began to erode because of Google and others. Running after Millennials and forsaking Boomers is a strategy. But the Boomers with lots of discretionary income (*Bloomberg BusinessWeek* calls them Generation Rich)[3] and empty nests will take their business somewhere. The leaky bucket analogy is real. You will always lose current customers, and you will always need to gain new ones. You must focus on doing both very well.

Failing to Keep the Brand Relevant

A brand is a dynamic entity that is affected by what happens in the world around it. A brand must be kept relevant. This does not mean changing its core essence. It does mean finding ways to update the way in which the core essence is delivered. Somehow either there is a push to bronze the brand delivery and experience or a push to completely change the brand essence. Neither of these is correct. A brand has an essential core that should be protected and evolved to make it relevant. However, as the world turns, so must the experience recognize the new world ways and determine how to stay fresh and vital. We should never abandon a core promise, but we can update the way that promise meets the customer.

Price Segmentation Instead of Market Segmentation

Price segmentation is not customer-centric unless you see your customers as a financial institution. Price segmentation makes things clear for the industry but is of no help to a customer making a decision. We talked about how the lodging industry still falls back into price segmentation. But customers do not feel they are purchasing an entry-level luxury experience. Price classification is not customer-driven segmentation. Customers want to know if the product or service will solve their problem, satisfy their need, and be right for their situation. Price segmentation is generic marketing. And perpetually focusing on price reinforces the persistent commoditization of the brand. To be brand based, you need to have a customer-based view of the marketplace.

Thinking the Lowest Price Is the Same as the Best Value

Low price and best value are not synonymous. Focusing on low price reinforces the idea that there are "value-conscious" customers versus "nonvalue-conscious" customers. This is not the case. Everyone is a value-conscious customer. The customers buying a large S-class Mercedes think it is a good value for them. Considering their situation, they believe this vehicle is the best value to satisfy their functional, emotional, and social needs. Likewise, the customers buying the Kia think it is the best value to satisfy their needs. The customers shopping at Target for an engagement ring think the value is excellent, and so do the customers shopping at Tiffany's. Remember the Trustworthy Brand Value equation: cost relative to the total brand experience multiplied by trust.

Failing to Instill a Quality Mind-Set

A quality mind-set is critical. To grow trust, we need to grow quality. Quality is not what we promise and not what we intend to provide. First of all, low price is often perceived as a sign of poorer quality. So fixating on price alone can hurt a brand's quality perception. Second, quality

---

is more than a statement about "good quality" ratings. Quality is not a test or an audit. It is a cultural mind-set, not a measuring stick. Quality is more than a yes/no checklist of items. It is not a department. Every employee needs to believe in providing a quality experience. Somehow quality is shunted off to its own separate area in operations, but it needs to be integrated into every part of the organization.

There is only one definition of quality. It is the experience customers expect and receive. That is the only reality. Living up to customer expectations consistently is how we increase perceived quality. Marketers do not decide quality; customers do. A commitment to quality must permeate every part of an organization's culture. It must be in our brains and in our veins.

Silo Mentality

We spoke of silo mentality at great length in this book. Silos are deleterious to brand health and for organizational health. They create all sorts of bad behaviors, such as hoarding, stopping the spread of ideas, internecine conflicts, and reinforcement of the status quo. This is not feudalism because there are no fiefdoms. Silos are for storage, not sharing. They reinforce lack of accountability for business results; it is always the other silo's fault.

We talk a lot about Integrated Marketing. But integration cannot happen when we build our organization on segregation. It is organizational sectarianism. Losers accept the segregation of the marketing function; winners do not! Break down the isolated towers of segregated responsibilities. The power of alignment is awesome.

Focusing on the Short-Term Rather Than Creating a Short-Term/Long-Term Strategy

This is how business stops and how brands are hurt. It's all about generating revenues in-the-year-for-the-year. Short-term leaders say, "wait until next year." The problem is that if you do not get ready now for next year, there will be no next year. Short-term leaders say, "For this year we will focus on incentives; we will stop it next year." Incentives are like addictive drugs; once you start, it is difficult to stop. In the meantime, you harm your brands doling out deals.

Not Sharing Across Functions, Geographies, and Brands

We live in a sharing economy. Somehow this should apply to business not just trends. The companies that are doing well because they leverage sharing are not just start-ups: these are straight-up recognitions of how our world wants to behave. It is a changing perception of ownership. It is a mutuality of spirit that exists. And, yet, in the organization, sharing is anathema. People believe their job will be diminished because sharing means loss of control. This must change. Organizations have a lot to share. If at the very least, sharing information and data will save money and other resources. If your organization has multiple brands, and if these brands are differentiated in relevant ways, then sharing information with a sibling brand is not aiding and abetting the competition.

Believing the Regions Are Not as Sophisticated as the Center

The center of the organizational universe knows best. Those in the center have better career tracks and are smarter marketers and strategists. This happens to be the thinking in many organizations, and it is unfortunate. This attitude cannot be continued. Being in the "field" is essential because that is where the action is; nothing happens until it happens at retail regardless of whether that retail is virtual. We had one client who loved being in Australia because it was the farthest point from the center. It was as if he was insulated from the central attitude and the CEO office. Through sharing and collaboration, leaders and managers can learn the possibilities of all jobs in all corners of the world.

Believing That Brand Management Is All About Marketing Communication

In some business schools, Integrated Marketing winds up in the school of journalism and becomes defined as Integrated Marketing

Communications. Integrated Marketing is much more than just communications. And, when taught in an MBA program, the approach is often formulaic and uncreative. (Elon Musk, PayPal, Tesla, SpaceX brands say, "At my companies, our position is that we hire someone in spite of the MBA not because of it." And, Scott Cook, at Intuit, says, "When MBAs come to us, we have to fundamentally retrain them....")[4] The result is that the primary role of marketers often becomes managing, executing. and evaluating marketing communications.

Integrated Marketing involves the integration of every customer touch point. It drives product and service innovation, customer experience design, service experience, and customer relationship management. This is all marketing. A narrow view of marketing devalues the value of marketing. The result may be to also devalue the importance of the marketing function in the executive suite. Effective marketing is not merely about message and media management; it is at the core of effective business management.

Allowing Data to Decide

Real, meaningful, actionable insights will not come from superior data analysis. There are too many marketers who believe that superior analytics will reveal superior decisions. Data analytics have an important role. Analytics provide input into decision-making. They do not make the decisions. People do. MBA has come to mean, "Manage by analytics." Marketing leaders must be more than reporters of the results of data analysis. We are evolving into a generation of marketers who live in an antiseptic, analytic world. Superior analysis provides understanding of where we are and how we got there. It does not provide insight into what kind of future we can and should create for our brands. Analysis alone will only tell us how to defend the status quo.

Linear thinking analysts are ineffective because customer behavior is not linear. Winners are nonlinear creative synthesizers. They draw together information from multiple fields and use that to create an understanding of why people do what they do and why people feel what they feel. They see creative patterns where others see disconnected fragments of information.

Endnotes

1. Harrison, George, "I Got My Mind Set on You," *Cloud Nine*, 1987; originally written by Rudy Clark, 1962.

2. Solomon, Steven Davidoff, "As Sears Gasps, Lampert Turns to Financial Engineering to Revive It," *New York Times*, November 12, 2014.

3. *Bloomberg Business Week*, "Generation Rich," November 24–30, 2014.

4. Furr, Nathan and Dyer, Jeffrey H., "Leading Your Team into the Unknown," *Harvard Business Review*, Vol. 92, No. 12, December 2014, pp. 80–88.

13

Guiding Principles

Some folks trust to reason
Others trust to might
I don't trust to nothing
But I know it come out right

—The Grateful Dead[1]

Guided Decentralization is like playing in a band. Everyone has her own instrument, her own sheet music. Sometimes there is exceptional improvisation and creativity, but it always winds being a harmonious interpretation of the same song within the same song's framework. Guided Decentralization as actualized in The Collaborative Three-Box Model leads to Brand Harmonization across geography and function. It's the same song with beautiful orchestration but not always the same notes.

Adopting and adapting The Collaborative Three-Box Model and creating a Brand Business Scorecard require a mind-set change throughout the entire organization. For it to work properly, bad habits should be tossed aside. The entire organization needs to be aligned around the building of trustworthy valuable brands. Mind-set change will happen when behaviors change. The first behavior to be put into place is collaboration, not command and control.

People are invested in their established ways of making the system work for them. There is a natural hesitation to reject any approach that provides a discipline requiring behavior change. People need to learn that having a common thought process does not mean common thoughts. People must realize that having actions based on the brand regardless of function and geography does mean giving up some individual power. It means gaining the power of the group. Effective collaboration means working together better and breaking down the functional silos and department fortresses.

Effective collaboration is a growing social development. The *Financial Times* reported on a "bubbling trend" in Eastern Europe describing the individual "post-communist youth" rebelling against the "aging political elite" who have changed nothing for decades. This youth movement is joining their separate grass root movements into larger, more national-based groups..."loose collections of urban movements" banding together for a bigger prize. One of the leaders said, "I noticed there were a number of these small local movements trying to stop urban developments. Now, we understand that waging many separated local struggles is pointless and we need to change the law and this can be done only at the national level."[2]

The Collaborative Three-Box Model does not destroy the organizational system; it helps dispose of the obstacles that make the system and the brand(s) stagnant. It replaces an antiquated, stultified approach with a vibrant, relevant way to manage brands in a changing world. This new marketing approach is a challenge to the hegemony of old-think brand management. It engages global, regional, national, and local leadership, instilling a system-wide openness, forward-looking, active participation. At the same time, it puts everyone on the same track for driving the brand toward its common Ambition. To make The Model work, it is necessary to put the aging hierarchical global brand management approaches aside and ditch the default behaviors.[3]

Signing on to this new method for global marketing is an imperative for global branding. Each organization is different. Each has its own established systems and structures.

Following are eleven guiding principles to make the transition more of an evolution than a revolution.

1. Define the Common Ambition

Before doing anything, the common Ambition must be clarified and communicated throughout the organization. Organizational alignment begins with committing to common goals and objectives. Everyone needs to know what the brand is trying to achieve. What is the destination? How is it defined? Why is it important?

By collaboration, we mean working together better to achieve a common Ambition. One client was concerned that having a common Ambition did not take into account the different stages of development of their global brands. This is not true. Having a common Ambition means that we are all headed in the same direction to the same goal. However, some countries may well be in different places on the road to the common Brand Ambition.

2. Clarify Roles and Responsibilities

To help achieve the common Ambition, people need to know what the center does, what the geographies do, and what they need to do as individuals. Job descriptions and reporting systems need to be clear. Each function in all geographies will have different responsibilities. At IHG, when we began The Collaborative Three-Box Model in practice, organizational restructuring and revised job descriptions affected hundreds of people around the world. It is important to ensure that the right people are in the right jobs doing the right things in the right way.

3. Realize That Brand Leadership Is Global; Brand Management Is Regional/Local

Brand Leadership is responsible for inspiration, education, support, influence, and evaluation. Global Brand Leadership is responsible for the "commonalities" across geographies that give the brand its core meaning. This means the common promise, essence, measures, language, knowledge gathering, issues, policies, and programs, including the common website. Regional and Local Brand Management are responsible for bringing the brand to life *within* the global brand framework, including relevant local differences in products and services, local innovations, local communications, local promotions, local digital implementations, and local retail initiatives. The center must learn how to lead, and the regions must learn how to manage with accountability.

4. Build Trustworthy Brand Value

The customer's new perception of brand value is already happening. When customers trust strangers and rating sites as well as the content generated by "friends," it is time to readjust the outmoded value equation that does not include social benefits, the cost of effort, and the trust multiplier. For example, Kik, a social chat-app, has 40% of Americans ages 13–25 using it on average 97 minutes a week. It is developing robots that chat to users about their preferred brands. This bot can engage with trusted conversations with users about brand.[4]

Adopting Trustworthy Brand Value as the new value equation has a huge effect on marketing. What are the drivers of the new equation for your brand? How do I grow each one of the new equation's elements? Help your teams understand the importance of this new brand value assessment because it will impact current pricing strategies.

5. Establish Cross-Functional Teams

Cross-functional teams (CFTs) are an excellent means for subtracting silos from the system. Silos are for grain. In fact, the word *silo* comes from the Greek *siros*, directly translated as *corn pit*. Silos are where grains are compressed airtight and stored. This is what those inside the silos do with ideas from the outside: isolate from everything. Insulated within a functional or geographic silo, managers tend to reject ideas that do not originate with them. These "silo chaperones" live a life dedicated to guarding rather than growing. They are the wardens of a way of weak, weary management that is not healthy for the company or the brands. Silo chaperones are great at containing, insulating, and protecting their own practices, theories, and approaches that have worked for them in the past but may not be effective in a changing world.

Caught in the whirlwind of globalization, localization, and personalization, a business needs new ideas and actions, not stale methods stored in isolated, organizational corn pits. Silos are also used for containing and occasionally launching missiles, and that is what silo chaperones do when they feel under attack by the apparent threat of collaboration. CFTs are changing how we cooperate and collaborate. It is the de-isolation of crucial functions on behalf of the brands. The Collaborative Three-Box Model cannot work without the connectedness of a

CFT. As a rule, silos should be eliminated and replaced by collaboration and sharing.

6. Acknowledge That Great Ideas Do Not Care Where They Come From

Ideas are a powerful resource. When a great idea is unleashed, it can move mountains or governments. In a world of instant information, the movement of an idea is without friction even if its outcome is friction. Ideas exist everywhere. It is arrogance or jealousy when the ideas from outside of the center are rejected out of hand. The regions and locales are the closest to the customer. Their ideas about the customer reflect a truer sense of actuality. "What rules the world is ideas, because ideas define the way reality is perceived."[5]

The Collaborative Three-Box Model opens the door to the spread of ideas. McDonald's advertising agencies in 2003 were asked to compete for the idea behind the brand essence of "Forever Young." A small satellite agency of a bigger U.S. agency in Unterhaching, Germany, had the winning idea. The idea led to the development and worldwide implementation of "i'm lovin' it," which became the longest-lived campaign idea in the history of McDonald's. Yet the most discontent and resistance to a creative idea from a small German agency came from the U.S.-based headquarters of McDonald's and the Chicago agency.

This attitude is not productive. Good ideas are everywhere. It is not the size of the country but the size of the idea that counts. The old-fashioned One-Box or Two-Box Models are based on the concept of ideas emanating from the home office (in fact, empires have been built on this concept) and then being disseminated to the local geographies to execute. But in today's world, this approach does not optimize the creative assets of a global organization.

7. Share the Knowledge

Share the wealth of organizational and brand knowledge. Along with eliminating silos through the development of CFTs and breaking down the barriers to accepting ideas from everywhere, sharing knowledge and experience is a third element for becoming a true learning organization.

Knowledge itself is important, but people need access to it.[6] It is quite painful to sit in a meeting and hear a manager say she has information, but it is on her laptop that's not accessible to anyone else. Or an executive might say that a particular level of employee or individuals cannot have the data because it is too important, they will misuse it, or they will not understand it until the data's owner explains it properly. Maybe people are told it is too soon to reveal the data because it is work in process or is not yet a success. Organizations do share success stories and so-called "best practices." But they bury mistakes and failures. The real failure is that the organization fails to learn from the mistakes of others.

An organization cannot claim to be part of the "knowledge economy" if it does not share knowledge internally. Yet management turns a blind eye to those who hoard information and data hounds that keep brand data "private" for safekeeping.

As reported in *Strategy & Business*, overseas employees transferred home tend to keep their learning to themselves. Only 67% of the 4,108 skilled returnees interviewed said they shared knowledge upon their return. Only 48% reported shared knowledge and then saw the knowledge implemented. "This means that on average, for every two workers with international experience hired by a given firm, only one will successfully share knowledge from overseas at some point during his or her tenure."[7]

The Collaborative Three-Box Model offers many opportunities for the data, information, and insight to be open to all. It is safer to spread the information around than keep it as the property of a single person. When an information hoarder leaves the company, the learning leaves as well.

8. Implement Brand Journalism

Everything communicates. Advertising is only one form of communications. Other things that communicate include store designs; public relations; "green" behaviors; packaging; service interactions; point-of-sale displays; websites and apps; and all images, sound, smells, tastes, and textures.

Today, many marketers still think about advertising and other traditional forms of content as the primary types of communication that build brands. Brand Journalism is about the whole spectrum of touch points that help build a multidimensional story for a brand across time.

A brand is much more than a simple, single word. It is a complex, multidimensional idea. How do we communicate the complexity of the brand in a consistent, coherent manner? How do we tell the brand story? Brand Journalism addresses the issue of having multiple messages while maintaining the integrity of the brand. It is based on the awareness that it is no longer possible to have a single, oversimplified message everywhere and still be a viable branded entity anywhere.

Brand Journalism requires collaboration across functions and geographies. It is implicit that the brand retains and maintains its core essence and everything within the Brand Framework. The creativity of Brand Journalism happens within the Brand Framework. As the world moved to digital, mobile, always-on, 24/7, techno-focused Brand Journalism evolved to provide a rationale for managing brand communications. Brand Journalism is still evolving, and it's doing so in such interesting ways.

In November 2014, Airbnb, the residential-sharing travel company, launched a print magazine called *Pineapple*. It is 128 pages featuring articles on three cities (cities favorable to Airbnb). In its introductory preface, *Pineapple* said that its purpose is "to explore our fundamental values: sharing, community and belonging" and to "inspire and motivate exploration, not just within the cities featured, but within any space a reader finds themselves."[8] It is a perfect message for the Age of I: inclusiveness and individuality. Find your own space, and then share and belong! And it is a perfect way to expand the brand's core while speaking to a specific target: Airbnb hosts. It is a modern example of an application of a journalistic approach to brand communications. Deutsche Bank has done a similar thing by launching a print magazine called *Konzept* designed as "a new way of delivering our best ideas to clients and the wider world." *Konzept* "aims to deliver fresh insights and ideas by pushing contributors to gaze beyond their core disciplines."[9]

9. Build Trust Capital

Organizations have many valuable assets. Managing these assets is usually handled by the C-suite level—where you find the CEO, CFO, CIO, Chief Legal Council, head of HR, and so forth. Organizational wealth tends to focus on Human Capital, Financial Capital, and Intellectual Capital. We add a fourth resource of value: Trust Capital. Of an organization's four wells of wealth creation, Trust Capital is important in our changing world because it connects and capitalizes on the intersection of three forces of globalization (standardization), localization (differentiation), and personalization (relevance).

Building Trust Capital means doing what you say you will do when it comes to promises made to all stakeholders. Increasing belief in the trustworthiness of the organization deposits trust currency into the corporate trustbank, and this builds Trust Capital. Large stores of Trust Capital secure future competitive advantage for the firm and for its brands. And building Trust Capital builds brand loyalty. Especially today when people are providing data about their experiences to unseen others (even bots) and taking "risks" with unseen parties online, trust is essential. If the site is perceived to be trustworthy, the customer commitment increases. Lucy Kellaway of the *Financial Times* sees this trustworthiness as a first lesson of learning about business from eBay. Trustworthiness, as she reports, is built into the eBay business model through ratings of sellers and buyers.[10] It is the same with the Uber business model as reported in *Harvard Business Review*. "The service relies on peer coordination between drivers and passengers, enabled by sophisticated software and a clever reputation system. Passengers rate drivers, but drivers also rate their passengers—building trust and promoting good behavior without the need for a more onerous rules-based system."[11]

Trust is also important internally. Employees want to believe that their leaders are trustworthy. Whether we are employees or customers, we have grown tired of surprises. Customers are increasingly demanding and skeptical. Trust Capital helps to eliminate the concerns that creep into our minds with each brand decision or employment decision we make.

To be trusted, brands have several major groups to think about: influencers, advocates, customers, and employees. Building Trust Capital influences the perceptions of each of these.

Transparency is so important in our open, easy-access, knowledge-sharing world. Increased emphasis on transparency is becoming more relevant in building Trust Capital. It is only a matter of time before the public discovers the facts about any issue. More and more companies are committing to being more transparent in their operations and communications. It is easy to rely on traditional advertising to tell someone what a brand stands for. It is more convincing when others tell the story on the brand's behalf. And it is even more convincing when people can learn the truth for themselves.

Currently, McDonald's has been fighting various rumors that undermine its brand credibility. In the spring of 2012, McDonald's Canada launched a marketing campaign called "Our Food. Your Questions." as a way to provide transparency about its foods. The ask-me-anything approach involved thousands of regular Canadians. Questions ranged from, "Are the hamburgers made from 100% real beef?" to "Are the hamburgers made from 'pink slime'?" McDonald's posted replies online, either with text or a behind-the-scenes video uploaded to YouTube. In 2013, McDonald's adopted a similar approach in Australia. In 2014, McDonald's adopted this approach in the United States.[12]

10. Institute a Brand Business Scorecard

Measuring overall brand business success keeps the brand and its leaders and managers focused on the Brand Ambition and how much progress is being made toward achieving its goals. Measuring and rewarding people for producing the right results and doing it the right way create a powerful brand-building culture.

A good Brand Business Scorecard provides all the information about the critical elements for driving forward on the road to enduring profitable growth. It evaluates global brand health and guides priorities. The Brand Business Scorecard is a great tool for becoming a learning organization because it highlights successes and failures. We learn what we should keep doing and what we must stop doing. We see where we can improve. The Brand Business Scorecard is also a way for everyone to learn about what others are doing across brand and across geography.

11. Allow Freedom within the Framework

The Collaborative Three-Box Model thrives on the freedom of thought and action on behalf of the brand generated by the ability to be creative within the Framework. Freedom within the Framework expects the regional and local teams to stand up for the brand by creating ways in which to localize and personalize the brand within the boundaries of the global givens. In fact, to not do so is to shirk responsibility.

Freedom can be frightening. Within the Framework you have the responsibility to do what you believe is right. Freedom can make you feel like a motherless child, make you feel like you are almost gone, a long way from your home.[13] And yet, that is the beauty behind Freedom within the Framework. The Framework is the support, the guardrails ensuring that you do not go off a cliff. The Framework gives you the courage to accept and act on accountabilities you now own. The collaborative nature of The Three-Box Model institutionalizes global sharing, knowing, and giving and frees those closest to the customer to bring the brand to life while respecting the global brand.

Endnotes

1. Garcia, Jerry, "Playing in the Band," *Workingman's Dead*, Ice Nine Publishing, 1970.

2. Foy, Henry, "Young Rebels with a Cause Take on Region's Aging Political Elite," *Financial Times*, November 12, 2014.

3. Hill, Andrew, "The Default Mode for Managers Needs a Reset," *Financial Times*, November 11, 2014.

4. Kuchler, Hannah, "Teenage Favourite Kik Raises $38m in Venture Funds," *Financial Times*, November 20, 2014.

5. Kristol, Irving, *Foreign Affairs*, Vol. 87., No. 4, July/August, 2008, p. 126.

6. Nagl, John A., *Learning How to Eat Soup with a Knife: Counter-insurgency Lessons from Malaya and Vietnam*, University of Chicago Press, Chicago, 2005.

7. Wang, Dan, "The Untapped Value of Overseas Experience," *Strategy & Business*, Issue 77, Winter 2014, pp. 14–17.

8. Levere, Jane L., "Airbnb Is Introducing a Print Magazine for Its Hosts' Apartments," *New York Times*, November 17, 2014.

9. Mance, Henry, "Deutsche Reaches Out to Clients with New Magazine," *Financial Times*, November 26, 2014.

10. Kellaway, Lucy, "Enroll Here in My eBay MBA," *Financial Times*, August 26, 2014.

11. Hiemans, Jeremy and Timms, Henry, "Understanding 'New Power,'" *Harvard Business Review*, Vol. 92, No. 12, December 2014, pp. 49–56.

12. www.yourquestions.mcdonalds.ca.

13. Havens, Ritchie, *Freedom*, 1967.

Conclusion: Moving Forward

"Would you tell me, please, which way I ought to go from here?"

"That depends a good deal on where you want to go to," said the Cat.

"I don't much care where—" said Alice

"Then it doesn't much matter which way you go," said the Cat

"As long as I get somewhere," Alice added as explanation

"Oh, you're sure to do that," said the Cat, "if you only walk long enough."

—Alice in Wonderland[1]

As we began in the Introduction, The Collaborative Three-Box Model is a new marketing approach, discipline, and mind-set. The learning in this book reflects the global work we have been involved with for many clients over many years across many industries. We helped to institutionalize some of the precepts and methods such as Brand Framework, Brand Journalism, cross-functional teams (CFTs), and Freedom within the Framework. This book pulls together the elements of our recommended approach into a coherent, ordered, creative, global, and regional process.

We are big believers in the problem-solution approach to marketing. The Model comes from years of working with clients. It also comes from our experiences as clients and observing from the inside the barriers that force organizations into unproductive behaviors and attitudes. These problems are reviewed throughout this book and in Chapter 12, "Bad Habits That Inhibit Brand Building," and include hoarding, not

---

sharing data; price segmentation over market segmentation; believing the regions are not as sophisticated as the center; and the silo mentality.

This new approach is a way of marketing global brands in an extremely and increasingly complex environment. The Model is flexible and responsive to changes on the global and the local level; it is not for those who embrace the status quo. Our cultural, social, economic, political landscapes are already in a state of change, and these movements will become even more prevailing as time goes on.

Demographics affect more than just marketing; they affect the way countries operate. Between 2010 and 2030, China's workforce is expected to lose 67 million workers according to the United Nations' projections. China is experiencing a low birth rate even with the revisions to the one-child policy; only 804,000 couples applied for the dispensation.[2] Countries with older populations behave differently. They take fewer risks, and they tend to keep things as is. They have fewer soldiers and tend toward different military and security arrangements.[3] Some economists including Larry Summers of Harvard University call this "secular stagnation," whereby countries fall into a "malaise" based on weak demand and excess savings, dampened growth and interest rates, and a smaller work force. The culprit for all of this is an aging population.[4]

At the same time, we have a huge population of Millennials in their twenties and early thirties. This group is creating new ways of communicating, relating, living, and behaving. Unlike the Boomers who wanted to reject and overthrow everything, Millennials want to keep things but change them according to their own wishes. Apparently, this applies to relationships, where "more and more Millennials are shying away from physical encounters and supplanting them with virtual quasi relationships: less casual sex than casual text."[5] Woodstock this isn't. (The *New York Times* reported that a UN Report says there are more adolescents—1.8 billion youths ages 10–24 years old—today than ever before in human history. This unprecedented number of youth will have huge ramifications for the countries in which they live.[6])

This demographic juxtaposition of Boomers and Millennials is a rare opportunity for brands and marketers. The older group is living longer and has more discretionary income. The younger generation has excitement and energy and is morphing all they touch into things they are happy with.

Regardless of how different these two groups are, they both want increased personalization. Whether this personalization is delivered via technology, via a human, or some combination of these, the demand for a more personalized experience is increasing. Preferred Hotels & Resorts and its sibling Preferred Boutique are advertising, "Luxury is always personal."[7] Sony is introducing a web-based TV service that creates a personalized, searchable way to watch live and on-demand television with its PlayStation Vue.[8] Spotify is now going to be available in Uber cars so riders can personalize their riding experience. "More and more people are skipping even owning their own cars and going straight to Uber, so this is a way for us to reach a younger and a Millennial audience in the cities," says Daniel Ek, CEO of Spotify.[9]

However, there is a dark side to personalization that brands and their owners will have to master, as reported in the *Wall Street Journal* article "Americans Say They Want Privacy But Act As If They Don't." The fine line between privacy and the privilege of being personally catered to is different from person to person. In fact, the report indicates that young people are just as likely to care about privacy trespass, if not more so when it comes to government surveillance.[10]

Personalization is just one of the changes that are creating The Age of I: the inclusivity and individualization of life and living. Strategies will have to consider how to simultaneously address the desire for uniqueness and belonging. We examined the self-sorting into unique, individualized communities of like-minded others across the United States.

Taken to its limits, "The Age of I" is redefining family into kin groups and kindred spirit groups. Now we have our families of origin (born into or united through marriage, adoption, and so on) and our families of communities of people who share our values, interests, opinions, travel destinations, love of animals, and so forth. Each one of these family arrangements represents a network of people. Strategies designed to communicate with a person's networks should build the brand if managed correctly.

And, for all people, there is a frightening decline in trust. We explained how serious this loss of trust is and how essential it is to focus energies on the customer's new value equation: Trustworthy Brand Value. Additionally, corporate brands must focus on a fourth source of organizational wealth: Trust Capital. Trust is not about how big you are but about how big you act. Openness, frankness, and social responsibility will add to credibility and integrity, adding currency to the company's trust bank.

These trends are changing our brands. Surrounding these trends are the three forces that are changing marketing: globalization, localization, and personalization in a modern-day *Clash of the Titans*. Globalization has been the brunt of a lot of negativity and is still the go-to wedge issue for many politicians. As *The Economist* stated, "But let political leaders everywhere tell their publics the truth: the years of easy post-war growth are gone, replaced by competition that cannot be wished away, and so must be met head on—and ideally harnessed."[11] In the same issue was another view of globalization.

The Economist also reported on a recent study, *The DHL Global Connectedness* Index, led by one professor from The Stern School of NYU and one from IESE. The study was based on data from 140 countries that account for 99% of the world's GDP and 95% of its population. The study shows that after a big post-crisis drop, the trend of growing global interconnection resumed last year. Globalization is back. The Index uses four types of cross-border flow: trade, information, people (tourists, students, and migrants), and capital.[12]

As globalization and the demand for global brands grow, localization and personalization grow with them. These three forces are on a collision course, and from our perspective, Trustworthy Brand Value is in the center. Building, increasing, nurturing, and measuring Trustworthy Brand Value is the only way to survive the confluence of these conditions. Each of these three forces has positives and negatives. But it is no longer a viable solution to take one or two of these into account. Now it is necessary to manage and maximize all three at once. Understand how each contributes to your brand's Trustworthy Brand Value. What is each one of these forces doing to the brand to face these head-on?

The Collaborative Three-Box Model tackles the three forces of Boxes 2 and 3 and allows for global and local and personal investigation and imagination. The Global Brand Framework must reflect the global world but be both big enough and tight enough to allow for the creativity needed for localization and personalization.

This is why our new approach to marketing global brands is the best way to address the forces of localization and personalization while keeping the global brand flame alive and resonant.

Endnotes

1. Carroll, Lewis (Charles Lutwidge Dodgson), *Alice in Wonderland*, Macmillan, UK, 1865, Chapter 6.

2. Burkitt, Laurie, "No Baby Boom After Shift in One-Child Policy," *Wall Street Journal*, November 8–9, 2014.

3. Goldstone, Jack A., Kaufmann, Eric P, and Toft, Monica Duffy, eds., *Political Demography: How Population Changes Are Reshaping International Security and National Politics*, Paradigm Publishers, NY, 2008. Also, Jackson, Richard and Howe, Neil, with Rebecca Strauss and Keisuke Nakashima, *The Graying of the Great Powers: Demography and Geopolitics in the 21st Century,* Major findings of the Report, Center for Strategic International Studies (CSIS), May 2008.

4. Free Exchange, "No Country for Young People," *The Economist*, November 22, 2014, p. 72.

5. Wayne, Teddy, "Swiping Them Off Their Feet," *New York Times*, November 9, 2014.

6. Sengupta, Somini, "Global Number of Youths Is Highest Ever, UN Reports," *New York Times*, November 18, 2014.

7. See advertisement in November 2014, *Travel & Leisure* magazine.

8. Steel, Emily, "Sony to Introduce Web-Based TV Service," *New York Times*, November 13, 2014.

9. Mishkin, Sarah, "Spotify Looks to Grab a Ride with Uber," *Financial Times*, November 18, 2014.

10. Miller, Claire Cain, "Americans Say They Want Privacy, But Act As If They Don't," *Wall Street Journal*, November 13, 2014.

11. Lexington, "The Nostalgia Trap: Politicians Need to Stop Pretending to Angry Voters That Globalization Can Be Washed Away," *The Economist*, November 15, 2014.

12. Free Exchange column, "Signs of Life: Despite Some Recent Reversals, There Is Evidence That Globalization Is On the March Again," *The Economist*, November 15, 2014.

Index

D

E

F

X–Z

W